HOW TO
thrive
as a
SMALL-CHURCH
PASTOR

Also by Steve R. Bierly

Help for the Small-Church Pastor

HOW TO
thrive
as a
SMALL-CHURCH
PASTOR

A Guide to Spiritual and Emotional Well-Being

Steve R. Bierly

ZONDERVAN™

GRAND RAPIDS, MICHIGAN 49530

ZONDERVAN™

How to Thrive as a Small-Church Pastor
Copyright © 1998 by Steve R. Bierly

Requests for information should be addressed to:

Zondervan, *Grand Rapids, Michigan 49530*

Library of Congress Cataloging-in-Publication Data

Bierly, Steve R., 1955–
    How to thrive as a small-church pastor : a guide to spiritual and emotional
well-being / Steve R. Bierly
       cm.
    Includes bibliographical references.
    ISBN 0–310–21655–9
Small churches. 2. Pastoral theology. 3. Clergy—Psychology. 4. Clergy—
Religious life. I. Title.
BV637.8.B56 1998   97-32368
    253'.2—dc21   CIP

Interior design by Sherri L. Hoffman

Printed in the United States of America

01 02 03 04 05 06 /❖ DC/ 09 08 07 06 05 04

To

John VanderTuin who taught me
that our God is an awesome God

Al E. LaValley who taught me
that it's a sign of strength to
admit one's weakness

Candace Lawrence, Crystal Etzel,
and Doug LaBudde, Jr., who
have saved my life more times
than I can count

My parents, James and Jean Bierly;
my children, James and Abigail;
and my wife, Deborah, who are
always anchors of love and sanity
in the sometimes chaotic seas
of ministry and life

Contents

Acknowledgments

Thanks to—

- Jim Ruark of Zondervan, without whom this book wouldn't exist.
- Herb Miller of *Net Results* and David Goetz of *Leadership,* for publishing my thoughts and observations on the ministry and thereby encouraging me.
- The elders and deacons I have worked with at Cobblestone Church, for their understanding and support.
- Dick Brian Klaver, for his friendship and the walks and discussions that sparked some of the ideas in this book.
- My brothers and sisters in the Alabama–West Florida Conference of the United Methodist Church, whose enthusiastic response to my seminar and warm Christian fellowship gave me added incentive to finish this book. Also, they introduced me to "field peas" and "poundings."

The stories you are about to read are either true, or composites of true stories, or based on what is real life for many small-church pastors. Only the names have been changed to protect the innocent—and the guilty, for that matter.

Introduction

My name is Steve. And I am a small-churchaholic.

At first I didn't think I had a problem. Oh sure, I occasionally took my job too seriously, but who doesn't? And, yes, when I was on family outings, I would sometimes have to let my mind sneak back to my congregation. After all, I told myself, a shepherd doesn't abandon the sheep. It was all part of being a faithful pastor.

But then things began happening that I couldn't so easily explain away:

— One night, I woke up at three in the morning, shaking, in a cold sweat, and screaming, "The new doors in the sanctuary have to be brown! Do you hear me? BROWN!"

— I found myself utterly depressed over the fact that a prominent woman in the congregation hated me. Never mind the fact that, as far as anyone could remember, she had hated every pastor and 98 percent of the members the church had ever had.

— Any accomplishments in my ministry faded to insignificance because I hadn't yet been able to persuade beloved Joe Inactive to come back to the church.

— I was consumed with guilt because I had forgotten to pray for a woman's sister-in-law's mother's brother as I had promised to do.

— During the NBA finals, I talked about the church all the way through a crucial game I desperately wanted to see.

— I no longer felt I had a significant part to play in God's plans for his kingdom. The small church had my ambitions and dreams effectively contained within the confines of its four walls. My life seemed as if it was going to be bound up with the problems, concerns, and complaints of small groups of people forever. There was no escape. Even if I moved, chances were I'd wind up in another small church.

I finally admitted I had a problem. A problem that wouldn't be solved with a change in geography. What was needed was a change in me. I had to admit that the small church was taking over my life, completely dominating my thoughts and emotions. I was losing my identity to it. No doubt about it, I was close to cracking up. Having faced my weakness, I sought help and determined to get the monkey off my back.

The principles in this book helped me do it. Not that I have totally licked the problem. You see, there is no such thing as an ex-small-churchaholic; there are only recovering small-churchaholics.

Since you picked up this book, chances are good that you are a small-churchaholic, or know and love one. Or maybe you suspect that you might be on your way to becoming one. Picking up this book is a cry for help. It's a good first step. With the Lord's help, you and I can journey back to mental health together.

Join me, then, as we look first at the disease, then the cure.

PART ONE

The Warning Signs

Okay, one more time. This is
your brain. This is your brain
stirred up by small-church
ministry. Any questions?

ONE

The Way of All Flesh

Some burdens are common to all pastors. Let's examine them and pay particular attention to the ways they are carried by the small-church pastor. You will see how easily pastors can break under the strains of the ministry.

#1—The Ministry Tends to Isolate You from Others

Rats! I had blown it again!

I was enjoying a conversation with the affable, jovial man sitting next to me on the plane. We talked about our families, joked about the weather, and weighed the benefits and liabilities of living in various parts of the country. But then, he asked THE QUESTION: "So, what do you do for a living?" And I was stupid enough to tell him—"I'm a pastor." (There's got to be another way to say it. "I'm an educator." "I'm in Growth and Development." "I administrate a nonprofit organization.")

Suddenly, his face got red. He had been peppering his speech with some rather salty language. He abruptly lost interest in talking with me, answering my questions now with only a polite "yes" or "no." When the flight attendant came around with the cart, he asked me if it would be okay if he ordered a drink. It was obvious that in his mind I was no longer one of the guys. I was (cue the heavenly music) a *holy man*. And one has to treat a holy man differently.

My mind went back a few years to when I was a college student. Taking a bus trip, I found myself sitting next to an attractive young woman. She was being *extremely* friendly with me—until I told her I was studying to be a minister. She sat bolt upright in her seat and I could read her mind from the look on her face: "Oh, no! I'll never get out of purgatory now! I just tried to flirt with a priest!"

Your identity as a pastor erects a wall between yourself and others. Some who have had bad experiences with ministers will be waiting for you to lie to them, beat them over the head with a Bible, let them down, criticize them, or hit them up for a donation. One of the highest compliments a person with this mindset can pay you is, "You're okay—for a preacher." You have to resist the urge to respond, "And you're all right, too—for an accountant."

Others will view you as if you were a delicate and fragile knick-knack. They feel they must tiptoe around you for fear of breaking your communion with God. They will try to shelter you from the evils and day-to-day realities of life, thinking such things would shock, upset, and offend you. They don't realize that, like G. K. Chesterton's Father Brown, you became a minister precisely because you are well acquainted with the darkness in men's souls, not because you are trying to run away from it.

Still others will believe that you are something more than merely human. In their minds, pastors inhabit a higher spiritual plane than "normal" people do. Some will be genuinely surprised that you get discouraged, tell jokes, catch the flu, become weary, watch TV, or have personal problems. In fact, some don't want to learn these things about you. They won't get too close to you for fear their illusions will be shattered. They want to believe in something and that something is you! (By the way, this may explain why they pay you what they do—they expect you to be able to multiply loaves and fishes for your family.)

Speaking of your family, the ministry can even separate you from the ones who should be closest to you. Not only will your schedule ensure that you will spend a lot of time apart from them, but you will feel totally justified in doing so. After all, isn't The Lord's Business more important than playing dolls with your daughter or going to a movie with your spouse? And didn't Paul say all the servants of Christ should be single, anyway? If your family is feeling lonely or neglected, that's just the suffering they must bear for the sake of the Gospel.

Even when you have the time to spend with the family, you may find that you don't want to. You are so burned out from people contact that your spouse and children look just like another committee that wants a piece of you, more counselees to advise, or a group that wants you to work up the energy to "fellowship" with them. Like Greta Garbo, the reclusive actress, all you want is to be alone. Unfortunately, you may just get your wish.

As a small-church pastor, you will be alienated even more from others in your congregation, not only because you're a minister, but also because you are an outsider. Small communities are very suspicious of, if not hostile to, outsiders, particularly outside "experts" who have the potential to change the cherished status quo. You'll find yourself being kept at arm's length. Things you say will be taken with an extra large grain of salt.

Also, members of your congregation may not feel much of a need to get to know you on a personal level. The tenure of small-church pastors tends to be very short. Therefore, you're like fickle Aunt Mary's latest boyfriend. Why should anyone in the family bother getting to know him when, come this time next year, he'll be gone, replaced by someone else?

Your congregation will not realize that you need friends. They are a group that has a closed system of long-established relationships. When church members need someone to talk to, or have to find help in a crisis, or just want to go on a picnic with someone, they don't have to think twice about whom they are going to call. They'll call the same people they always have, the same people they always will. They have a ready-made support system. It hardly ever crosses their minds that you don't.

And when they do seek to include you, such attempts frequently backfire. At a church dinner, several families came over to my table to "chat awhile and get to know you, Pastor." Yet when the conversation began, they started reminiscing about their good old days together. "Remember old Mr. Johnson, our history teacher in high school? Remember the time you hid his precious pointer and he got so flustered he couldn't finish class? I wonder what ever happened to him anyway." Talk turned to a local tragedy I knew nothing about. "Yeah, the Smiths have to give up their farm. Too bad. I always liked them." The families then started making plans among themselves for the weekend. "I've been meaning to call you. Let's get together Saturday night and play some cards. The kids can play hide-and-seek out back." My wife and I felt as though we were invisible. We had wrongly stumbled into someone else's family reunion. We were like Ralph and Potsie on TV's *Happy Days* tagging along on Ritchie's date. And it hurt.

The small-churchaholic in me wants to dwell on the hurt and scream, "They purposely left me out!" But it's not true. They just didn't know how to include this strange creature called "the pastor" in their conversation.

#2—The Ministry Pressures You to Give Up Your Identity

I worked for several years in the "secular world" between college and seminary. Before I left to pursue my M.Div., I attended my college's home coming weekend and ran into an old friend, "Jack," who was already an ordained pastor. I was glad to see him and shouted out a greeting.

"Jack" turned slowly, with a dull, vacant look in his eyes. Instead of slapping me on the back and shouting, "Well, hi there, Bud" (my college nickname), he took my hand in a very careful, mechanical manner. Holding it with just the right amount of pressure (not too much or too little), he said in a rather flat voice, "Hello, Steve. It's good to see you again. Are you enjoying the weekend?"

I made a joke about the weather.

"Yes, well, it is a little uncomfortable. Still, we can't complain too much. These things are in the hands of the Lord."

At first, I thought he had to be putting me on. But as the weekend progressed and I observed him with others, it became evident that the man I had known was gone and in his place was now ... ROBOPASTOR! His personality (not to mention his vitality) had been submerged beneath layers of artificial programming designed to make him "The Ideal Minister." Once in a while, the real man would break through for just an instant. When that happened, he would become nervous, and quickly the ROBOPASTOR programming would assert itself again.

I left the gathering shook up, mourning for my lost friend, cursing the forces in the "Christian" church that could so obliterate a soul. I hoped that, like Officer Murphy in the movie *Robocop*, somehow he could become an individual again.

As I entered the ministry, I began to experience firsthand the kind of pressure that my friend must have endured. I was continually prodded to conform to the standards of others in many areas of my life.

It started in seminary. One of my professors asserted that *each* minister *must* spend ten-to-twelve hours preparing for *every* sermon or else he or she is shirking one's duty. This, of course, ignores the fact that some people work faster than others. Or that public speaking comes naturally to some but is hard for others. Or even that in the real world of the church, there are weeks so filled with counseling and crisis situations that you only have time to give the sermon a lick and a promise. I've known pastors who burned the midnight oil on Saturday, not because they didn't have a decent message ready to give, but because they felt they hadn't put in their time. I heard a famous pastor say that he had once told his congregation that he didn't have a sermon for them that week because he hadn't had the time to prepare a message "with integrity." I wish I could get away with that!

Another teacher hammered home that all sermons must make three points (no more, no less) and that all points must begin with the same letter. Regardless of the fact that I don't write or talk that way, at least I could fill up my designated twelve hours trying desperately to come up with the needed alliteration!

A New Testament professor told us not to accept a call to any church that wasn't near a theological school because "a good pastor will spend much of his or her time in the library." Aside from condemning most country churches to pastorless oblivion, the professor was actually telling me where I had to live!

My peers were no better. I was associated with a group of ultra-conservative Reformed students. When a new book by a Reformed author appeared in the bookstore, the word went out that this was something we *all had to* buy. Certain speakers came to campus and certain forums were offered that we *all had to* attend. Other speakers and forums we *all had to* avoid. Woe to anyone of us who thought that a Reformed speaker had lost a debate or who admitted that non-Reformed speakers made some good points.

Pressures to conform only intensified when I graduated and moved "to the field." I quickly learned that nearly everyone in a small local church has set notions about what a pastor is supposed to be. Most people aren't afraid to let you know where you fall short. Of course, what can threaten your sanity is that, at times, no two people will agree.

— "The last pastor always stopped in for a cup of coffee with me one morning a week."
— "Our previous pastor never did anything to move us forward. He just spent all his time chewing the fat with our members."
— "A pastor should be involved in at least one community organization as this shows the town that you care."
— "Too many outside activities, and the church will feel like you're neglecting them."
— "As our pastor, we need you to lead."
— "I hope you're not going to be one of those pastors who is always telling us what to do."
— "You're called primarily to be our preacher and teacher."
— "Do you mean to say, Pastor, that you haven't bought the Advent candles yet?"
— "We want you to have the time you need to refresh yourself physically, spiritually, and emotionally."
— "I'm in my office every morning at nine, whether or not I've had a late meeting the night before. I don't see why you can't do the same. When I drive past the church in the morning, I expect to see your car there."

If you minister in a small town, you'll discover that the entire population has certain expectations of you, too. For better or worse, you can't hide out in a crowd in a small town. Everybody knows you are the pastor. When you go out to your mailbox in shorts and a T-shirt, inevitably someone will drive by, honk the horn, and wave. The small-churchaholic can't help but worry, "What did he think when he saw me dressed this way?"

I am a fan of movies and comic books, but there are times I've passed up picking up a copy of *Rolling Stone* to glance through its excellent movie reviews for fear that someone will see *the pastor* touching, to say nothing of reading, such a magazine. I've steeled myself to walk past racks of comics in supermarkets and book stores because I know that Batman and the Incredible Hulk aren't supposed to be on the pastor's recommended reading list.

On those rare occasions when I, as a small-churchaholic, turn my attention to the larger universal church of Jesus Christ, I find even more pressures to conform. In the mail I receive brochures from "experts" in the ministry who let me know that they have discovered the perfect way for my church to grow numerically and spiritually (a pretty neat trick considering that they know absolutely nothing about me, my people, or our area). If I will only come to a three-day seminar and be programmed . . . er, I mean, trained, then I can return to my parish and plug the program in . . . er, I mean implement the plan, and success in the ministry will be mine. What am I waiting for? Why don't I send in the money now?

Books and professional journals offer me conflicting advice on the ministry. Some urge me to be the visionary, take charge, CEO of my church. Others tell me to give up the organizational reins and concentrate on being a spiritual director. One advocates preaching "seeker-sensitive" sermons, another commands me just to preach the plain, unvarnished, old-fashioned Word of God. One says that my closest friendships must be formed with people outside the church in order to protect myself. Another counsels that my best friends should be the leaders of my congregation.

Who should I listen to? Should I listen to anyone? What am I as a pastor supposed to be or do? How do I know whether adopting someone's suggestions will lead me to become more the minister God wants me to be, or instead, squeeze me into a mold that doesn't fit? In the case of my friend, "Jack," the life had been squeezed right out of him.

#3 — The Ministry Tells You Lies About Yourself

— "Steve, you are the kindest, most gentle and loving man I've ever met. And your messages are always just what I need to hear to get me through the week."

— "Steve, unless you do something about your temper you'll never amount to anything in the ministry. Why, in last week's sermon you even took out your anger on the congregation. That message was nothing less than Satan's tool to divide the church!"

— "Steve, God is going to use that sermon to spur us on to revival. He really spoke to my heart."

— "It was all I could do to stop from walking out in the middle of your so-called message. It was the most insensitive, disgusting thing I've ever heard."

Now, for a little test. These statements to me were:

(a) Made by members of the same congregation, reacting to the same worship service.

(b) Made by people in the same age group and the same socio-economic class.

(c) Made by professing Christians, active in the life of the church.

(d) Lies told by well-meaning people who didn't realize they were exaggerating.

(e) All of the above.

And the correct answer is e. To some people in the congregation, I'm the closest thing to Jesus on the face of the earth. I don't go to my office. I ascend to God's throne room to sit at his right hand for awhile. I never make mistakes. Certainly, I never sin. And I've never had an "off" day or preached a less than inspiring sermon in my life.

To others in the church, I'm nothing but trouble. I wouldn't recognize God's will if he wrote it in the sky for me in blazing letters. I don't give myself 100 percent to the ministry and *it shows*. I don't care about my people. I'm in danger of going to hell, let alone washing out of the pastorate.

I would be in deep trouble if I believed either of these extremes. And in the small church, I'll hear both of them. I'll definitely be notified of the opinions of everyone and, as a small-churchaholic, I can brood over them for hours or days or weeks. In recent years we've all heard about pastors who got themselves into deep trouble. They probably took the opinions of others too seriously.

Perhaps they listened to those who told them that they were always right about everything. Consequently, they led their churches into financial ruin pursuing some half-baked vision without counting the cost or listening to other opinions.

Perhaps they loved the attention and affection of the "pastor groupies" so much that they ignored their spouses. Perhaps, listening to critical, sometimes even demonic voices, they became depressed and drowned their sorrows in alcohol, pornography, or drugs.

Perhaps some, feeling like they have sincerely tried to serve God and, from what everyone's telling them, have blown it, decide to go willingly down a path of destruction in order to put as much distance between the Lord and themselves as possible. Any of these things could happen to you. And you're lying to yourself if you think they can't.

You're also deceiving yourself if you think that no one else on earth knows the suffering you go through. "Nobody knows what it's like being a pastor. There's nowhere to turn for understanding and solace. Oh, the cross we leaders are called to bear!" We like to believe that we are such martyrs for the cause of Christ. The truth is that there are many professional men and women in this world who experience living in a "fishbowl"; unexpected emergencies; recalcitrant individuals; having to be "on" at a moment's notice; seeing some souls you've worked with pour their lives down the drain; public criticism; trying to give advice to those who may not want it;

and hectic schedules. What about doctors and nurses, teachers, politicians, social workers and police officers, to name just a few? It's easy to build up in your mind a picture of yourself as a unique, noble, tragic hero when really you're just a typical public servant. The temptation for the small-churchaholic is to equate bumping into a parishioner at the mall on your day off with bearing in your body the marks of Jesus. It can be inconvenient, embarrassing, draining, or even annoying. But it's just part of the job.

#4—The Ministry Can Reopen Old Wounds

I have a war injury that flares up from time to time.

One of my people can come up to me after a worship service and say, "Pastor, nobody really knew that last hymn that you picked out this morning," and suddenly, my stomach begins to hurt. My mouth gets dry. My hands become clammy. Why? I'm remembering that in a former parish a major conflict began with people finding "little things" wrong with my ministry. Although this member of my current congregation isn't going to make anything out of this, mentally I'm waiting for the boom to be lowered.

The trouble is that the pastorate can keep me so busy that I never have time to adequately care for or recover from my old wound. And, being paid the salary of a small-church pastor, I own no mountaintop cabin to which I can retreat. So I continue on—at best, slapping another bandage on the wound in order to keep going. It never fully heals. It's always a little tender, just waiting to be bumped or scraped and start oozing pus again.

Other old aches and pains can surface to give me problems.

Sitting with a family grieving over the loss of a loved one, I can once again experience the pain of losing my grandparents. Preparing a sermon on controlling the tongue, I replay the things I've said during the last week which may have been hurtful. Teaching a parenting seminar, I can be reminded of the fact that I really haven't been spending enough time with my own children. Counseling someone on how to conquer a specific sin, I can become burdened with the knowledge of how strong that temptation is in my own life. Listening to the life stories of my parishioners, I can get caught up in reliving the broken relationships, unfulfilled dreams, wrong choices, and periods of despair and confusion in my personal history. Stressing the importance of time alone with God to new members, my heart can sink as I remember that my own devotional life is "on hold."

There is also a danger that pastors can spend so much time navel gazing that we forget to look up and pay attention to where others are. In some ways pastors have to be like the medics in M*A*S*H, able to put aside our personal discomforts in order to give the wounded our best. Certainly pastors should empathize with their people (Romans 12:15) and be able to comfort others with the comfort they themselves have received (2 Corinthians 1:3–4). Interacting with others should sharpen us (Proverbs 27:17), lead us to realize and forsake our sins (1 John 1:8–10), and move us on in the process of spiritual growth (Philippians 3:12–14). I have, however, found myself tuning out counselees while I start once again looking inward at my own heart. I want to say to them, "Yeah, yeah, yeah, you've got problems. But wait until I tell you mine!"

#5—The Ministry Leaves You Open to Temptation, Which in Turn Leaves You Feeling Like Slime

Whenever a member of my congregation switches to another shift at his or her job, usually it's only a matter of time before he or she makes an appointment to see me with one or more of the following complaints:

— "I just don't feel close to God anymore. Half the time I don't even know if I'm still a Christian or not."
— "I can't seem to control my temper. Everyone around me irritates me, including my family."
— "You wouldn't believe the X-rated thoughts I've been having. I can't stop them!"
— "Lately I've been feeling, what's the use of anything? My life is never going to get any better. I'm stuck in a hopeless rut."

Satan is a master at spiritual warfare and one of the rules of warfare is, "Hit your enemies when they are at their weakest." When a person's mind and body are trying to get used to a new schedule, he or she is in a weary, weakened state. Those hungry sharks—the world, the flesh, and the devil—move in for the kill.

Pastors often find themselves working all shifts at once—having meetings that run late into the night, taking early morning phone calls, counseling and visiting people in the afternoons, and feeling at all hours day and night Paul's "pressure of my concern for all the churches" (2 Corinthians 11:28). Of course, the small-churchaholic can't ever slow down or take a break from the job. So, the sharks will smell blood and they circle around. You're shocked at just how easily you can fall:

— "I can't stand my people. If I get one more phone call from one of them I'm going to scream!"
— "God should be everything I could ever want, but right now *I need chocolate!*"
— "While I counseled that young woman, my thoughts kept returning to how great she looked in shorts."
— "How can I urge others to believe God for something big when, after last night's board meeting, I don't even feel that he exists anymore?"
— "I can't see any evidence that I'm changing anyone or anything with my ministry. This church is never going to grow and I'm doomed to live out the rest of my years in ecclesiastical obscurity."

After you've been tempted, or worse, have given in, the demon shark attacks are most fierce. They will try to rip the meat right off your bones. They'll munch away:

— "How could you, God's messenger, say what you just did? Aren't you supposed to be the spiritual leader of this congregation? If your people followed your example, they'd be marching right down into hell behind you."
— "How dare you preach to others about holy living when you can't even control yourself?"
— "Where's the Spirit's power in your life? Hmm? A pastor without the Holy Spirit—Ha! What a laugh!"

— "Hey, man or woman of God, blow your stack one more time for us. You're so cute when you're doubting and blaspheming."

And on they will continue, unless you can chase them away (see part 2 of this book on how), or until your spiritual life and vitality are eaten up and nothing is left but dry bones.

#6—The Ministry Brings You Face-to-Face with the Overwhelming Presence of Evil in the World

There I was—a grown man afraid of the dark.

I didn't want to enter that sanctuary by myself at night. I kept thinking of all the petty bickering and back-stabbing that had gone on in that small congregation for years. I thought about the opposition I was encountering as I presented the gospel. Suddenly, I realized that I wasn't afraid of the dark. I was scared of The Darkness. There seemed to be an aura of evil, maybe even a spirit of some sort in that place. I wasn't experienced enough to deal with it. A shiver ran down my spine. The hair stood up on the back of my neck. Now I knew that there was a presence inside that sanctuary waiting for me. It was bad enough that it ambushed me every Sunday morning as I stood in the pulpit. I always felt a heavy weight descend on me. It was as though I was preaching through a dark cloud. I felt dizzy, nauseous, about to pass out. By the grace and power of God alone, I always managed to get through the worship service and some lives were touched, but the negative spirit of the church remained the same. Prayer vigil or no prayer vigil, there was no way I was going in there for half an hour by myself in the dead of night. I hurried out of the building, jumped into my car, and headed for home.

The demonic realm is all too real for the pastor, more so than for the average Christian. This may be because we have to think about it more than others do. Not only does the Good Book I study warn me about it, but people keep bringing it to my attention, whether I want them to or not.

There's the parishioner who used to dabble in the occult before she was converted and now feels an evil spirit invading her house in order to terrify her from time to time. There's the man who told me that he saw the angel of death as he was out walking the dog, and that evening, someone in the neighborhood died. Or the man who felt that a dead relative paid a visit to him one night. I may not be the *X-Files* Agent Mulder, but I hear my share of spooky stuff (from rational, credible people) just the same.

Such stories and thoughts invade my subconscious. Every once in a while I have what I call one of my "demon dreams." In it, not only are devils trying to destroy my ministry, but they take control of friends and loved ones in an effort to kill me. I usually wake up right about the time they are either pouncing on me or starting to possess me. I used to think I was cracking up until an older pastor whom I greatly respect confessed to having such dreams, too. In fact, he told me it was an "occupational hazard." He himself can't watch any scary movies or even listen to Christian testimonies about "power encounters" of demons being cast out without feeling a black dread settling over him. He then finds himself afraid to get out of bed at night, sometimes for weeks at a time!

The demonic realm is also very real to pastors because we see first hand the damage it does in people's lives. A pastor passed out while visiting a young man in the hospital emergency room. It wasn't the blood and stitches that got to the pastor. He had seen these types of things before. The young man had been driving his car over one hundred miles per hour, resulting in an accident and crippling the girl who had been riding with him. The pastor reflected on the sick, dysfunctional family life which had led the young man to that point, the tragic and senseless mangling of a young life, and the prison time which the young man would almost certainly do. He was overcome with the realization that the forces he would have to fight in order to bring God's grace into the situation were enormous. He felt so helpless. The next thing he knew, he was on the floor.

I can relate to that pastor. When people are telling me their histories and confessing their sins, I sometimes find myself listening to such sordid tales of abuse, sexual perversions, violence, greed, selfishness, and hate that it's all I can do to keep from running out of the room and throwing up.

Every night the evening news sorts through the garbage of the world and spews out the most tragic, disgusting, and vile tidbits it can find into our living rooms. Some people can turn it off and forget all about it the next day at work. In the pastorate, you are constantly being shown the garbage. You can start to believe that's all that exists in the world. You know that God is supposed to triumph over Satan, but it sure seems as though the wrong side is winning. You've seen counselees backslide, stubborn board members stand in the way of new and needed programs, people leave the faith when the going got rough, and innocent people devastated by the actions of others who seemingly get away scot-free. Where was God in all of that? Is he in control or not?

Pastors are also painfully aware of how everyone eventually ends up. They spend their careers trying to prepare people to meet their Maker. They visit the dying, officiate at funerals, and comfort the grieving. Pastors know that anyone can go at any time. They've gotten phone calls in the middle of the night informing them someone once seemingly healthy is now dead. Pastors start to wonder, "Who's next?" Especially when they are ministering through a "season of death." Remember the old saying, "Bad things happen in threes?" Well, amazingly enough, they often do! Funeral directors have told me that deaths seem to occur in waves. One had even charted "death trends" and informed me, "We're in for a busy year, Pastor." During that kind of year, you can become preoccupied with death. A sense of doom follows you around. Will you or your family be next? You find yourself remembering the words to the old song you used to sing when you went through your "gross" phase in junior high. Only this time you're not laughing:

Did you ever think when a hearse went by
That you might be the next to die?
They wrap you up in a big, white sheet
And drop you in a hole so deep. . . .

In the small church, death and evil have faces. I don't just preside over the funeral of a parishioner, but of someone I've come to know. The pastor isn't just concerned about violence in our society;

he or she is concerned that Karen's husband won't stop beating her. The small-church pastor doesn't just read the newspaper or call a meeting of the board in order to determine "what problems in the community we need, as a church, to address." The small-church pastor is intimately involved in the real day-to-day lives of flesh and blood people. This makes the suffering we observe that much more devastating. Because the small church views itself as a family, every crisis is then a "family crisis." For the small-churchaholic, ministry is often like having six relatives in the hospital at once, all demanding your attention and care. The thoughts of what they are going through stay with you long after you leave the sick room or the counseling appointment. Everyone's suffering becomes your own until you are worn to a frazzle.

#7—The Ministry Alienates You from God

Bzzt! Bzzt!

"Yes, Miss Johnson, what is it?"

"God's on line one, Pastor. He wants to consult with you about the direction the church should be heading."

"Well, look, I'm pretty busy right now. I've got a building committee meeting this afternoon and I still haven't prepped for tonight's Bible study. Tell him I'll try to work him in next week—sometime—maybe."

Your schedule can often be so crowded that you find you neither have the time, inclination, nor energy to be alone with God. You might find yourself urging others to love a God that you no longer have any affection for. There just hasn't been a chance to cultivate the relationship. You tell others to rely on God's power to get them through life while you yourself are doing the work of the ministry totally on your own strength.

It's so hard to seek the Lord. First, you have to quiet your spirit. (Ha! That's a laugh. Every time I try, the phone rings, and a small-churchaholic *has* to answer it.) Next, find a relevant Bible passage, then study and meditate on it. Finally, pray through an endless list of requests your people gave you. If only God would just send me a short, to the point, fax once in a while, everything would be cool.

Some might say to me, "Pastor, it must be wonderful to be in full-time ministry. Imagine getting paid to think about God all day long!"

Yes, but that's just the trouble. I'm being paid to think about God. He then becomes my *vocation*, not my *avocation*. Years ago, an interviewer remarked to a famous actress how lucky it was that she enjoyed exercise because actresses have to stay in shape. "Enjoy it?" she said, "I absolutely hate it! The only reason I do it is so I can keep making money. My job depends on looking like a movie star, so I've got to put in the hours. But left to myself, I wouldn't." I assume that at one time in her life, the actress must have enjoyed working out, or she probably would never have become famous in the first place. But over time it became something she no longer wanted to do, yet something she was made to do. Most pastors probably started out loving to contemplate God, or they wouldn't have become pastors in the first place. Now, though, something's changed. I do it because I gotta, not because I wanna.

Instead of being my Father and Friend, God is now my *Boss*. (And you know what they say about entering into business ventures with family and friends.) You no longer are working *with* God to build his kingdom, now you're working *for* God, in the worst possible sense. God becomes the one who is directing more counseling cases your way, giving you more organizational problems to solve, asking you to train leaders, and urging you to spend time in prayer for world missions when you already are feeling swamped. The Boss is really piling it on! And I'd better scramble to do a good job.

Workers joke about their bosses being omniscient. Mine actually is! He knows every time I flub up, every time I goof off. When I open up his memo to me (the Bible), it seems that I'm brought face-to-face with the fact that I and the department I head (the local small church) aren't living up to expectations. Sometimes I wonder why I put up with him. After all, in small churches he doesn't really pay all that well (at least not in this life). People at other jobs, with the same years of schooling I've had, putting in the kinds of hours I do, take home fatter paychecks. And now the Boss is saying he wants to spend time with me away from the job, wants to get to know me personally?

That'll be the day! Maybe I have to put up with Scrooge on the company's time, but after hours I'm my own man.

"Pastor, I envy you. You must see evidence in people's lives all the time that God is *real!*"

Well, yes, I do, but I also see things that could lead me to believe that God is *really* absent, or *really* not as active as we think he is, or *really* weird. For example, what am I to make of the woman who insists that God has cured her when she still has all the symptoms of her disease? Or what about the man who insists that God told him how to vote on a certain issue at the board meeting, even though he had the facts of the matter totally wrong? How about the woman, living in squalor, overweight, emotionally unstable and uneducated, who assures me that God has appointed her to be a prophet to our generation? And then there's the church that my friend once visited. The congregation maintained that it had proof that God's glory-cloud was resting on their building and they showed my friend the pictures to prove it. However, my friend is a photography buff and recognized "fog" on the film (a common problem) when he saw it. Not that such knowledge could dissuade the faithful, of course. Sometimes I find myself wondering, is God really with me, blessing me, guiding me, teaching me—or am I just off the deep end, too?

"But, Pastor, you get to spend hours on end studying the Bible! How exciting!"

Yes, and how frustrating. My hours of study have shown me that not everything in life is black-and-white and that there are at least two sides, if not more, to many theological questions and issues. My study often leaves me shaking my head in confusion, instead of bowing my knees in worship. Sometimes I wish I could return to the days when I was just "a simple believer."

I've seen my parishioners became unglued when I explained to them that there was more than one Christian view on such topics as the end times, women's ordination, and the role of the secular government. They think I'm trying to destroy their faith. "I thought the Bible only teaches one way! You're saying that the Bible can mean anything we want it to mean, that man can impose his own teachings on top of the Word of God!" Some counsel that if I'd only pray, God would tell me which interpretation of these issues was The Correct One. And of course, I would come to the same conclusion that they did because God had already told them.

I wonder how these believers would cope if they had to study to prepare this week's sermon? The liberal commentary I consult (because its data on the history and customs of ancient people is superb) tries to logically convince me that the story in the scripture passage couldn't really have happened. The priests just made it up to reinforce the values of the cult. The three conservative commentaries disagree with each other over what the main points of the story are. One feels that a Hebrew phrase contains certain nuances, while another says that this interpretation of the wording is all wet. I'd love to be able to preach the pure, simple, true, unchanging Word of God—if only I knew what it was.

TWO

Tempests in a Teapot

At the biweekly ministerial meeting, Pastor Tinygroup found himself sitting next to Reverend Biggerflock. Pastor Tinygroup began to share some of the struggles he was having in his ministry, particularly with one cantankerous Mr. Oldermember.

The Reverend Biggerflock interrupted, "You can't let anyone intimidate you. Remember, you're God's man with God's plan. Just show your congregation who's boss!"

Pastor Tinygroup thought, *But that's the problem, everyone already knows who's boss—Mr. Oldermember!*

The Reverend Biggerflock was on a roll. "You've got to dream dreams, set goals for your group, and then proceed full speed ahead!"

Yes, Pastor Tinygroup inwardly acknowledged, *I could do that if I could somehow get rid of my board. Besides, the last two pastors who tried to push things through in my church were sent packing.*

"Say, are you listening to me or not?" Biggerflock arched his right eyebrow.

"Oh . . . yes, of course. I guess I'm just tired, that's all. A woman from our congregation is going in the hospital for a tricky operation and I've been spending a lot of time—"

"Wait just a minute! Is she a potential leader in your congregation?"

"Well, no, but—"

"That's your problem. You've got to learn to spend 80 percent of your time with just 20 percent of your people—the ones who can influence others."

Pastor Tinygroup didn't say a whole lot after that. What was the point? Biggerflock couldn't really relate to what he was going through. Though Tinygroup and Biggerflock were both ministers of the gospel, it was obvious they lived, moved, and worked in totally different worlds.

There are mental burdens to bear that are either unique to the small-church ministry or are particularly heavy for the small-church pastor, as opposed to Reverend Biggerflock. Let's examine these burdens and see how they can threaten your health.

#1—The Small-Church Ministry Bogs You Down in Minutiae

Poll any group of pastors as to why they entered the ministry and I can guarantee that you won't find any who will say,

— "I became a pastor because I enjoy coaxing a broken copier into producing this week's bulletins."
— "I love being caught in the middle of long-standing feuds between picky, unforgiving people."
— "I enjoy mediating disputes over such earth-shaking matters as whether it's time for a church to purchase a new sign or what color the new hymnbooks should be."
— "I've always seen myself as a janitor. I really wanted to be the one who has to make sure the church building is unlocked whenever a group needs to use it."
— "I wanted to enlist people to run rummage sales."
— "I'm called by God to bug committee chairpersons to get their work done on time."
— "I'm a master at wrangling with zoning boards over new Sunday School wings and increased parking."

— "I'm desperate to receive phone calls asking me when the next potluck dinner will be, or if my congregation would be interested in purchasing the latest video series that's taking Christendom by storm, or if the kids in the youth group need permission slips to go on the retreat."

— "I aspired to be the branch manager of God's Complaint Department and I can't wait to defend why the service went ten minutes overtime last Sunday or why we use grape juice for the Lord's Supper instead of wine."

Yet pastors can find themselves spending a great deal of their time doing the above or activities like them. I can put in a full day's (and night's) work on the job and find that I haven't cracked open the Bible or said a prayer. I didn't need to. Many pastors secretly wish they hadn't spent their time in preparation for the ministry by learning dead languages and studying church history and had, instead, taken business administration, conflict management, and abnormal psychology courses at the local community college. Pastors find themselves facing jobs for which they have little or no training and, more importantly, in which they have no real interest.

Chances are good that you entered the ministry for any or all of the following reasons:

— You felt called by God to take his message to the world (Isaiah 6:8).

— You wanted to be a soul-winner and a disciple-maker (Matthew 28:19–20).

— You knew that God could use you as a teacher to prepare his people for works of service (Ephesians 4:11–12).

— You have received comfort from God and now want to pass that comfort along to others (2 Corinthians 1:3–4).

— You love leading worship (Psalm 34:3).

— You desire to help the poor and the suffering (Matthew 25:31–46).

— You have a passion to see justice done in the world (Malachi 3:5).

But now you find that your time is taken up with tasks and duties that seemingly have little to do with your aspirations. If you are an "aggressive" small-churchaholic, you will act like a race horse that is pent-up in a small stall for too long. You are unable to do what you were created, trained, and called to do, and so you go nuts. Man O'War kicks the walls of the stall. You lash out at the congregation that confines you. You snort, neigh, whinny, and bite.

Or perhaps, you are a "passive" small-churchaholic. You become more like a worker trapped in a "drudge job." Day after day you're on that assembly line while your heart is elsewhere. Knowing that you'll never really be able to follow your heart, something inside of you dies. The fire in your eyes goes out. Your body still shows up to work every day, but your soul is no longer there. You begin to live for bowling leagues, cable TV, and days off. The job merely pays the bills. It no longer excites or motivates your spirit.

#2—The Small-Church Ministry Puts You on an Emotional Roller Coaster

The small-church pastor has a lot invested in every tidbit of news he or she hears. Bill Hybels might not turn cartwheels over five new people joining Willow Creek, but five people may increase your congregation by 20 percent. Also, in the small church, you'll hear every piece of news instantly, because everyone has access to your ear. Jerry Falwell may have call screeners, but you have to jump out of the shower to get to the phone.

The pastor's heart is often like a Ping Pong ball, being hit by conflicting news reports and bouncing back and forth from agony to ecstasy in the space of a few heartbeats. Because the small-churchaholic feels somehow personally responsible for everything, good and bad, that happens to the church and everyone in it, he or she is doomed to manic-depressive cycles.

Your phone rings. It's that vibrant young couple who have been visiting your church. They've decided that they want to become members! Hurray! Now to talk them into—oops!—I mean, enlist them as youth group workers. The phone rings again. This time it's a woman in tears, devastated because her husband just left her. You not only feel for her, you share her confusion. This man is a leader in the church. There's a knock at your office door. In comes the treasurer with the news that giving is way down this year. "I don't know how we'll meet our budget," he sighs, "particularly when we have to pay all your benefits." He looks at you hopefully. You glance up at the ceiling. That afternoon, a note arrives in the mail thanking you for last week's sermon. The writer said it had been as if God was throwing her a lifeline through your words. Also in the mail is news from the denomination about an evangelism workshop coming to the area. Your heart starts to soar. This is just what your congregation needs! Then, suddenly, you come crashing back down to earth again as you remember the stony silence that always greets any mention of evangelism at the board meetings. The phone rings. It's your spouse. "Hi, Honey. I just thought of you and called to say, 'I love you.' How's your day going?" Good question. You wish you had an answer.

#3—The Small-Church Ministry Makes You Feel Like a Failure

You may be painfully aware of the fact that people in your congregation respect James Dobson's counsel more than they do yours. You know you haven't got the political clout of a Pat Robertson or a James Kennedy. You can't preach as effectively as Chuck Swindoll. Unlike Billy Graham, when you give an altar call, multitudes do not come forward. You're not Robert Schuller, so you can't book big name guest stars for next Sunday's worship service. And if you should ever forget that you don't quite measure up to the famous pastors of our day, never fear! There will always be someone in your church who will remind you.

A woman who routinely skips Sunday morning worship services because she's tired, or has other commitments, or whatever, lets me know that she *never* misses a certain preacher on TV Sunday nights because, "His messages are such a blessing. He's a real man of God. He knows the Bible backwards and forwards." What am I, chopped liver?

Another woman took me to task because I disagreed with her favorite media preacher on a theological issue. "Well, after all, Pastor, God blesses him. He's on TV and everything!" I fought back the desire to respond, "So is Bart Simpson. Does that mean you should listen to him?" Or less charitably: "If I could talk enough people into sending me twenty dollars a month, I could be on TV, too!" Or even *less* charitably: "Next time your mother is in the hospital, why don't you call your TV Super Star to visit her. After all, we want her to be *really* blessed, don't we?"

Aside from being made to feel inferior to "the competition" (whether media giants or "truly successful" pastors in your area), your job description is one that Jesus himself couldn't fill. As one older pastor said to me, sorrowfully shaking his head, "It used to be enough if you preached and taught the Bible, visited the people, prayed for the sick, and married and buried folks. But not anymore." And he's right.

Today's pastor is expected to: have an informed opinion on all the important issues of the day; be computer literate; know how to operate the sound system; interact in a meaningful way with the youth; be on call for crisis counseling twenty-four hours a day, seven days a week; "motivate us to do evangelism"; dream great dreams for your church; serve on the board of directors for the food pantry; keep foreign missions in the forefront of people's minds; come up with a plan to restructure the Sunday school department; help out at the church fund-raisers; get yourself known in the community; keep abreast of the latest developments in church growth and sacred music; familiarize yourself with current movies, TV shows, best-sellers, and hit songs, so as not to be irrelevant; explain the tax codes to the treasurer; make sure your building is handicap-accessible; write up a "sexual harassment" policy for employees of the church; organize support groups for people recovering from various types of abuse; save the environment; lead a stewardship campaign; picket the adult bookstores; heal broken marriages; deliver a powerful, moving sermon every week—"I come to church to be uplifted, you know."

No one person could do all of this. Intellectually, we know that. So why do we feel so guilty when we can't? Because small-church-aholics have a perverse need to feel horrible. We want to believe we're doomed to forever attempt what's absolutely impossible.

As a pastor, you've been called to take an unbelievable message to a skeptical, cynical world. Some pastor friends and I were talking about how outrageous the Christian faith is. We believe a carpenter who lived two thousand years ago was God. We believe that after he died, he came back to life three days later. We believe that one day our loved ones will rise up from their tombs with brand new bodies. We believe that the other religions in the world are wrong. We believe in seas parting, ax heads floating, men walking around in blazing furnaces, angels and demons, visions and dreams, and that a centuries old book filled with archaic notions has the right to tell us how to live our lives. I'm often aware that to nonbelievers, I must sound as if I'm trying to sell them the Brooklyn Bridge.

Not only is the message outrageous, so are the messengers. God wants to call the world to be reconciled with him and to do this he's chosen—*me?* Weak, tired, overworked, confused, sinful *me?* Like Moses, aware of my own shortcomings, I often want to say, "O Lord, please send someone else to do it" (Exodus 4:13). Like Paul, I often ask, "Who is equal to such a task?" (2 Corinthians 2:16). I know that I'm not. Yet, I've been called to do it anyway. Sometimes I feel as though I'm a five-year-old who's been given advanced calculus problems to solve. I'm just going to cry over and over again, "I can't! I can't!" And the teachers will yell at me, make me stay after school, or fail me again and again and again.

Repeated failures are the order of the day when the pastor tries to "move the church ahead." The small church is notoriously slow when it comes to making changes and adopting new ideas. The pastor's programs and plans are shot down by the board, committees, matriarchs, and patriarchs. After awhile, he or she lets them just die on the drawing board without mentioning them to anyone else. The small-churchaholic is scared of being discouraged, disappointed, and frustrated again. Then he or she starts to ask, "What kind of a leader am I if I can't get anyone to follow? How can I shepherd this flock when they refuse to be guided to where God wants them? Where's the power of the Lord which should anoint my ministry?"

As a small-churchaholic, I can't help but dwell on my failures. Then I start to wonder whether the woman who preferred the TV theologian to me may be right. If I'm such a great pastor, *why aren't I* on TV? If I'm really chosen and blessed by God, why am I stuck in this little out-of-the-way congregation? I can easily come to the conclusion that Jack Nicholson came to in *One Flew Over the Cuckoo's Nest:* "I must be crazy to be in a loony bin like this."

#4—The Small-Church Ministry Requires You to Do the Same Tasks Over and Over Again

Small churches aren't looking for Starship captains to take them boldly "where no one has gone before." They are quite content to stay right where they are, thank you very much. Instead, they want a chaplain who will be there when a word of comfort or counsel is needed, lead them in a worship service at the "chapel" every Sunday morning, and marry and bury them. The small-churchaholic, full of ideas on how to reach out to the community, improve the church's programs, restructure the board, and lead the congregation into the twenty-first century, isn't going to be content with being a chaplain. You want excitement and challenge, but this week's "to do list" is much the same as last week's. You've got to visit elderly Mrs. Shut-In yet again, prepare another Wednesday night Bible Study, work on another Sunday sermon, and stop by the Johnson's to welcome Tommy back from his appendectomy. Wouldn't you rather be working on all of those innovative ideas percolating in your brain? The small-churchaholic in you grows to resent the fact that you can't and that, even if you could, nobody would want to hear about them anyway. The ministry gets kind of boring. After awhile, you feel you could do the work of being this group's chaplain in your sleep. (On the bright side, this allows you to catch up on your rest while on the job.)

As a small-church pastor, you'll be dealing with the same people over and over again. Many will have the same needs from day-to-day, month-to-month, and year-to-year. And unfortunately, they'll also probably have the same eccentricities, personality quirks, and social graces, or lack thereof, time after time, too. Some will bring you the same complaints over and over. Small-church people don't easily let go of the past. This means that they can nurse grudges about real or imagined slights that happened long ago. And they'll speak of those slights with all the intense emotions usually associated with something that happened just yesterday. In one church I served, I always wondered when (not if) during each board meeting a certain member would bring up the fact that he felt the church had taken a drastically wrong turn when it invested its money in the stock market *fifteen years ago!*

The phone will ring. My wife answers and informs me its Mr. So-and-So. Inwardly I scream, *Oh, no, not again!* But, I get through it by doodling, daydreaming, or catching up on some reading as my caller blathers on. I don't really need to listen to him. I know what he's going to say. And then there's a sweet, well-meaning elderly woman who tells me *exactly the same stories* every time I take her the Lord's Supper. I know she can't help it, just as I can't help feeling very, very sleepy while in her house.

It takes a good long while for small churches to take action on anything. As pastor, therefore, you need to steel yourself to the inevitability that "repairing the shed out back" will be on the board's agenda for at least a year and a half.

The scenario will probably play out something like this:

At each meeting the question will be asked, "Who was supposed to take care of that thing?" Nobody will remember, so the minutes of the last meeting will be read. It will be discovered that Fred had been appointed to see to it. "News to me," Fred says, "but, yeah, I'll get it done by next meeting." Of course, he promptly forgets. At the next meeting the question is asked, "Do we really need to repair that thing? Why not just tear it down?" A long discussion ensues. It's decided that we really need to fix the shed, but that Fred doesn't have the time to do it. Any volunteers?

No? Well, think about it until next meeting. At the next meeting, another member will be appointed who will drag his heels. Finally, one Saturday, a member of the congregation will fix the shed because, "I'm sick of waiting for the board to do anything about it." The board will then cross the item off their agenda. The shed has been fixed—mission accomplished!

If variety is the spice of life, then the small-church pastor often feels that life is tasteless. The small-churchaholic begins to feel like the asylum inmates who spend every day doing the same thing over and over again, endlessly cleaning the same spots on the floor or bashing their heads repeatedly against the rubber wall.

#5—The Small-Church Ministry's Wounds Are Inflicted by Friends

I remember the pain and abandonment I felt when I found out that a small-church board, with whom I felt I had a good relationship, had been having secret meetings for some time about "what's wrong with the pastor." They had been smiling and patting me on the back for months, while at the same time trying to get rid of me.

Criticism in the small church comes not from "a certain group of people in the congregation," or from your colleagues during the give-and-take of staff meetings, but from people you feel are your friends. You've been working hard to get to know them, to become part of their lives, to be there for them—and now THIS? Since the small-churchaholic gives his or her love away so completely, the breakup of any relationship hurts intensely.

I couldn't believe my ears!

The young man had just accused me of not caring about him. This was after I had spent hours crying and counseling with him. No matter that I had once given up my family's Easter dinner (as any small-churchaholic would) in order to help him with a problem. But now, just because I had said, "No," to an idea he had for the church, suddenly he felt I didn't love him anymore. A short time later, he and his family left the congregation. I was hurt and angry. These people weren't just statistics on our year-end report.

They were people I had "bled" for. And they turned their backs and walked away! What a colossal waste of my time! What a colossal betrayal of my love!

The Bible says a lot about bearing up under persecution. Of course, its usually talking about persecution from outside the church. How does one bear up when one's enemies are *inside* the household of faith? How can you still believe that Christ loves you when Christ's body is out to get you or has seemingly abandoned you?

Turning to the church-at-large provides little relief either. More than one disheartened small-church pastor has been further deflated to find out that denominational bodies know that certain congregations are "seriously troubled," but fail to mention that fact to the pastors when they install them. Pastors are placed in situations where they are destined to fail! Why weren't these congregations ever disciplined? Well, it's better in the denomination's eyes to lose a few individual pastors than to lose entire churches. Besides, small-church pastors aren't really that important in the corporate, expansionist, spin-doctoring scheme of things so prevalent in some denominations. As one pastor wrote (I forget where), "If you think that you're ever going to get help from your local judicatory, dial 1–800–GET–REAL."

#6—The Small-Church Ministry Enlarges Tom Thumbs Into Goliaths

Every small church has its share of "big fish in little ponds." In fact, some people join a small congregation precisely because there they can become Shamu the whale and throw their weight around. In a larger body of water, they could jump, thrash around, blow bubbles, and leave nary a ripple on the surface. In the small church, everyone ends up wet. In the small church, King (or Queen) Shamu and entourage can compose one-fourth of your congregation! If they decide to swim away, they'll leave quite a gap to be filled (particularly if they were heavy givers and hard workers). Therefore, others in the school of fish always defer to them.

In one church I served, the start of the annual Sunday school picnic had to be delayed for an hour because starting before a

certain matriarch arrived was unthinkable. In another congrega-
tion, all decisions were put off until it was determined what
Harold and Bill wanted to do, because, I was told, "It's really
Harold and Bill's church, you know."

All small-church pastors soon learn that they had better please
the Emperors (to change the metaphor) or their days are num-
bered. In fact, small-churchaholics drive themselves crazy trying
to ensure that they will get a "thumbs up" instead of a "thumbs
down" from the powers that be. I can easily find myself hurrying
to greet the visitors on Sunday morning, not only because I want
to welcome them, but because I know an Emperor will ask me if
I caught them before they left. I might constantly bring up stewardship at the board meetings because I know it's an Emperor's
hot topic and I want to show him that I'm in there fighting for the
things he wants.

The Emperors and Empresses haunt small-churchaholics even
when they are not around. I can notice that a matriarch seemed
to be in a bad mood on a Sunday morning and spend the rest of
the week worrying about whether or not it was because of something I've done. I can see a patriarch seated with another church
member at the local coffee shop and *just know* that they are talking about me. I can hear stories of how the Emperors conspired
together to force the last pastor out and I dream that even now
they are plotting to overthrow me.

As a small-churchaholic, I'm no longer in control of my own
life. I've turned control over to *them*. I've made these mere mor-
tals into my gods. How much more of myself will I have to sacrifice in order to appease their anger or obtain their blessings?

#7—The Small-Church Ministry Can Make You Lazy

All things tend toward entropy and small-church pastors are no
exceptions.

I don't have to strain my brain much to do my job. I can dazzle my congregation with insights taken directly from my seminary notes or gleaned from articles and books read years ago.
Theologically, I'm already light-years ahead of most, if not all, of

my people. I know more about church history than most members of the congregation care about. When it comes to church-growth strategies, polity, and worship renewal, I know more than they want to know or will ever ask me for. Frankly, I know much more than my job in the small church requires. So, the temptation is just to coast. The problem is, like riding a bicycle, you always coast the fastest when you're going downhill.

The tendency to slough off and put my brain on hold isn't helped by the fact that small churches may not hold me to very exacting professional standards. Small churches are often happy just to have gotten someone to come and fill their pulpits. "At least we finally found a pastor!" Since the most important things to small-church people are relationships, not oratory skills, as long as you are friendly and a good listener, you can get away with murdering the English language from the pulpit. Also, small churches are often served either by people seeking to work their way up the ecclesiastical ladder or pastors with one eye on retirement. Therefore, small congregations may be used to having leaders whose hearts aren't fully into their work. I remember one small congregation constantly praising me for doing above and beyond what previous pastors had done, while all I thought I was doing was just my minimum job requirements!

Writing about the small-town (and also small-church) mentality, Kathleen Norris says, ". . . we resist all outside influences in order to make our institutions what we want them to be, and end up creating institutions that are mediocre and unstable."[1] It's hard for the pastor (the outside influence) to fight against that resistance and it's much easier just to be content with the mediocrity. Everybody else seems to accept the status quo. Why shouldn't you?

Once you make the decision to go along with the way things are, your intellectual and spiritual muscles slowly atrophy. And it will be very hard to get back in shape again.

PART TWO

Taking Back Your Marbles

An ordained mind is a terrible

thing to waste.

THREE

The Ecstasy in the Agony

I was with my kids at the Schenectady Children's Museum when a revelation hit me.

Small-church ministry is an optical illusion!

We were examining famous pictures which are actually two pictures in one, depending on how you look at them. You've probably seen the pictures I'm talking about. One can either be two vases or two faces looking at each other. Another is either a young woman with a fancy hat or an old crone. Suddenly, I realized that my ministry was exactly like those pictures. If I looked at it one way, it was a drag, a trial, a frustration, even a curse. But if I looked at it another way it was exciting, a chance for spiritual growth, a joy, and a blessing.

As a small-churchaholic, I, of course, had a vested interest in seeing my ministry in as bad a light as possible. That way, I could feel justified in being grumpy and depressed. I would have good reasons for abusing my body by staying up late worrying or overeating. And I didn't have to take responsibility for my actions. I did what I did because the job *drove* me to it.

However, after viewing those pictures I had to stop and wonder. Was the job driving me crazy, or was it my *perception* of the job that was driving me crazy? As Shakespeare said, "The fault lies not in the stars, but in ourselves." Or, if you prefer Pogo, "We have met the enemy and he is us."

So, I knew I had to try to view the various aspects of my job in as positive a light as possible. At first, I rebelled somewhat, thinking that this was more "positive thinking" than it was "gospel truth," but then I came across a Scripture that commanded me to view my cup as being half full instead of half empty. In Philippians 4:8, Paul writes, "Finally, brothers, . . . whatever is admirable—if anything is excellent or praiseworthy—think about such things."

Okay! Okay! God said it. I believe it. That settles it. Right? Right.

I took some of my main frustrations in small-church ministry and tried to see if there were other ways to look at them which would emphasize the things that were admirable or praiseworthy. I wanted to find the young woman in the fancy hat instead of the old crone.

It's Not Really "My Church"

I refer to the congregation I serve as "my church," but it isn't really. It belongs to those members who were here ahead of me. It belongs to those who are permanently settled in the community, the ones who will stay here long after I've moved on to another call. They are the ones who wield the power. I'm often a "leader" in name only. I don't have the authority to change the seating arrangement of the choir, much less the structure of the Sunday school department. I'm an outsider, trying to convince a close-knit group that, just maybe, a stranger might have one or two ideas that could help them. That is, of course, if those ideas aren't too radical and don't upset anyone. I can't lead by "casting a vision," issuing challenges, setting measurable goals, or hiring an "excellent" staff who will carry out my plans. Instead, I have to lead by cajoling, dropping hints, compromising, making sure the right people are on my side—in short, by playing politics. I know too well that I'm only in office by the sufferance of my electorate. If I displease enough of the right people, I'm history.

But is this state of affairs really as bad as it seems?

I attended a week-long seminar that featured pastors of huge churches as its speakers. One of these pastors happily told the participants that his church board was little more than a rubber stamp. The board always approved everything the pastor wanted to do, because, as he told them, "Gentlemen, it's my job to lead. Your job is to follow." Another pastor regaled us with tales of some of the outrageous stunts he performed in the pulpit to drive his sermon points home. Later, at lunch, a bunch of us were sitting at a table with one of his associate pastors. We remarked that it seemed to us that the congregation let Pastor X get away with murder. The associate replied, "You have to understand one thing about Church Y. Church Y is Pastor X's church. All the people who are attending there are coming because they like Pastor X and they want to see what he will do next. Pastor X holds the church together and if he ever left, I honestly believe the whole thing would fall apart."

They say that absolute power corrupts absolutely. Could this be one of the reasons we've seen big name Christians fall into sin, or make outlandish claims, or begin half-baked projects that they couldn't complete? Maybe they started believing their own press. Maybe they truly felt that they had all the answers and that every word that escaped from their lips was gold. In the case of the two pastors from the seminar, years later, the one with the rubber stamp published an article in his denomination's magazine denouncing many of the principles he taught at the seminar, saying that following them had nearly wrecked his ministry and his marriage. As for Pastor X, a friend of mine got a job as one of his associates. When my friend left his position, he sadly commented, "Church Y doesn't need the Holy Spirit. They have the amazing Pastor X, a brand new facility on prime property, a huge budget, and studies that show them exactly how to scratch the itches that residents of the city have. The Holy Spirit could leave Church Y today and they could continue to grow and prosper for at least five years before they'd even realize anything was missing."

In the small church, I will be spared the corruption that comes with absolute power. I will have my ideas challenged (even when I'd rather they weren't). But this is healthy. It will serve to keep me sharp. Proverbs 27:17 says, "As iron sharpens iron, so one man sharpens another."

In the small church, I will be spared the temptation to think that I am the indispensable man. The members of my congregation met together long before I arrived on the scene. The church won't close its doors after I leave. People here have covenanted together to be a congregation of the Reformed Church in America and to worship the Lord corporately on Sunday mornings. They haven't formed a "Steve Bierly" fan club. One of my recent joys in ministry was discovering that attendance hadn't dropped off during the three weeks in August I was away on vacation. One of the reasons for this is that the people seem to be falling more in love with God and with each other. They want to get together with their Father and their sisters and brothers in Christ whether I'm there or not.

No, it's not my church. But then again, that's the whole point. The church belongs to Jesus Christ. It's his bride, not mine. In the small church this becomes painfully clear. And I'm glad it does.

The Ultimate Volunteer Organization

The small church is a volunteer organization. The workers I have available may not have the experience, training, time, or resources necessary to ensure that everything we do is "first rate." This can be extremely frustrating, not only because we want to "give of our best to the Master," but also because we're told by the experts that unless a congregation can demonstrate "excellence" it will never grow. People today demand and expect "quality service," and if they don't get it, they take their business elsewhere.

To the contrary, I've seen individuals in small churches grow, even if new members weren't beating down the doors. I think of the young woman from an extremely troubled family who was sort of shy and lacking in some of the social graces. If a church was looking to staff its "excellent" children's program, surely she would never even be considered. Yet, she became a Sunday school teacher and found that, not only did she love it, but the kids loved her. Her confidence grew, as did her willingness to try out other areas of service in the church.

I remember, too, a young man who wanted to share his music with the congregation. I decided to let him. It turned out to be a painful experience for all concerned. He was so nervous he was shaking, his style wasn't quite what the church was used to, and his voice cracked (some would say "split apart") when he tried to reach the high notes. Yet, he eventually went on to head up the music ministry in another church. In a megachurch, he probably wouldn't have been given a second glance. He either would have failed the audition in front of the talent coordinator or been told that the slots on the praise-worship team were already filled.

The small church, out of necessity, lets people experiment with their abilities and discover spiritual gifts they never knew existed. In the small church, we may have to make do with what we have, but we often find that we have more than we imagined.

Keeping a Light Grip on Our Plans

Small-church ministry has an air of impermanence about it. As a small-church minister, you may be painfully aware that if you lose one or two more families, the congregation won't be able to pay your salary. You may be ministering in a part of the world that's seeing its businesses close, its young people move away, and its quality of life deteriorate. You may be pastoring a congregation of senior citizens and with "the way things are around here," you know there's not much chance that new blood will be introduced any time soon. You have faced the fact that in twenty years or less, the congregation will die, literally.

My wife and I are always asked by the small churches we serve, "Do you plan on staying here long?" Our answer is always, "We don't know." We would love to put down roots into a community and to have a place to call home, but we realize that there are too many forces beyond our control that could necessitate our packing up and moving on again.

As a small-church pastor, the future is out of my control. I can map out my week, setting aside time to work on plans for an evangelism campaign to win our area for Christ, when suddenly the phone rings. Mrs. Allen has been rushed to the hospital. It looks like a massive heart attack. Can I come right away? My week is then spent with the family in the hospital and, unfortunately, preparing for the funeral. Not that important ministry isn't being done, but it certainly wasn't what I had planned. Over time, I can begin to give up on the idea of making long-range plans at all. Each time I do, something happens to disrupt them.

But, actually, the small church forces me to do what the Bible requires—keep a very light grip on my plans. James 4:13–16 says,

> Now listen you who say, "Today or tomorrow we will go to this or that city, spend a year there, carry on business and make money." Why, you do not even know what will happen tomorrow. What is your life? You are a mist that appears for a little while and then vanishes. Instead, you ought to say, "If it is the Lord's will, we will live and do this or that." As it is, you boast and brag. All such boasting is evil.

The small church keeps me humble in that it constantly reminds me that my time is not my own. I'm not in charge of my destiny. The Lord is.

And the Lord is in charge of a congregation's destiny, too. We may think we have our church's future all mapped out, but suddenly, a major illness can hit us, finances can dry up, or our new building can burn down. We need to acknowledge that our best-laid plans amount to nothing if the Lord is not behind them. Instead of patting ourselves on the backs for the ingenuity and hard work that brought the church to where it is today, we need to get on our knees and thank God for the life, breath, energy, training, and gifts that he has used to build his kingdom. And we need to ask for his continued presence as we face the future.

A feeling of impermanence may not be so terrible to live with after all. In fact, it may be one of the keys to wisdom. Ecclesiastes 7:2–4 says,

> It is better to go to a house of mourning than to go to a house of feasting, for death is the destiny of every man; the living should take this to heart. Sorrow is better than laughter, because a sad face is good for the heart. The heart of the

wise is in the house of mourning, but the heart of fools is in the house of pleasure.

The impermanence of small-church ministry probably won't allow me to build a monument to myself here on earth. Instead it will urge me to lay up treasures in heaven, the only permanent home I have. All good things come to an end. The small-church pastor knows this and can be prepared for what comes *after* the end.

A Ministry to Friends

Earlier in this book, I mentioned the frustration that comes in the small-church ministry from having to deal with the same people over and over and over again. However, when I roused myself from my small-churchaholic stupor, I saw that there are many blessings to this as well.

The small-church ministry lets me be myself in that I don't have to try to think and act like a pastor when significant milestones occur in the lives of my people. I can just do what comes naturally because, in the small church, I really know the members of my congregation.

When I'm doing a funeral for one of them, I am doing a funeral for a friend. I'm not just reading the words of some generic funeral service. I'm searching the Scripture for words that will comfort people I love. I don't have to put on a suitably sober face and adopt a mournful attitude. I'm actually in mourning! Likewise, when I'm doing a wedding, I don't have to force myself to be joyful. I'm happy and ready to celebrate. Two people that I have laughed and cried with are being joined together in marriage! In the Reformed Church in America wedding liturgy, the pastor asks the family and friends of the bride and groom to take vows to support the new couple. At this point in the service, I feel like stepping off the platform and taking the vows, too. Performing a wedding is not just another task of the ministry for me. It's asking God's blessings on my friends.

While I may get discouraged when I see some church members wrestling with problems that just won't go away, I also have the privilege of seeing growth occur in people's lives, too. I'm not just handed a progress report from my counseling staff, "One hundred thirty people have been helped this month." I get to see marriages being healed, sins being forsaken, men and women sobering up. I remember one woman telling me that she just had a good talk with her sister and was looking forward to seeing her soon. I rejoiced! Why? Because this woman had a history of holding grudges and clinging to past hurts. When I had arrived at that church, she cornered me and had gone on and on about the number of times her sister had done her dirt. Now, a couple of years later, she was ready to forgive. And she seemed to think my sermons and Bible studies had something to do with her change in attitude. Praise the Lord!

I remember a young couple, living together with no immediate plans for marriage, attending our church and over time becoming convicted that what they were doing was wrong. I married them and later gladly baptized their baby. And you couldn't wipe the smile off my face the day the husband was ordained as a deacon.

I once saw a young bride opening presents at her wedding reception drop everything to start reading the new study Bible she had received. She had to be told several times to put it down and open some other gifts. I felt like crying tears of joy! Not only because a young person was so hungry for the Word of God, but also because I knew some of the spiritual pilgrimage that had brought her to that point. These are moments when God has shown me that he's touching individual lives through my ministry. As Fred Astaire sang, "They can't take that away from me." In fact, such times are often what keep me going. I can be totally bummed out by a conflict in the church. My small-churchaholism can be in such full swing that I barely feel like a Christian, much less a pastor. But when I look out Sunday morning and see the faces of people I care about, people who have touched me as well as people I have touched, I feel energized again. Suddenly, it seems so right to be in that pulpit that I can't imagine doing anything else.

Not only am I getting to know and love the members of my congregation, but they are getting to know and love me. Because of that, I'm freed from the pressure to be perfect. During the worship service, I sometimes will mix-up my words. I've also been known to blithely skip over a part of the service without being aware of what I've done. Nobody really complains. They know that when I get tired, I make mistakes. And they know that if I'm tired it's because I've spent the week immersed in their concerns. A wise older pastor once said to me, "If your people know you've been with them in the trenches all week, they'll overlook an occasional bobble on Sunday morning." Besides, the people are coming Sunday morning to worship God with their friends and to hear the Word of God preached by a friend. They aren't coming out to see this week's show. I really feel like I'm sharing with them, not performing for them. They aren't going to demand a ticket refund if the extravaganza didn't meet all their expectations.

Once, when I was a practicing small-churchaholic, I lost my temper at an individual during a board meeting. I, of course, immediately felt like slime, but I apologized. To my surprise, the apology was accepted and we moved on. The board members knew that it hadn't been the 'real me' talking. It was the disease. As it was, many of them had experienced mild cases of it from time to time and knew exactly what I was going through. As friends, we were able to quickly put the matter behind us. They accepted me, warts and all.

And I learned to accept them, warts and all, too. This is probably the main advantage in being a small-church pastor—you've been put into a situation where you have to learn to love a diverse group of people over a prolonged period of time. If I were the pastor of a baby boomer church, I wouldn't get a chance to learn the depths of love that I learn in the small church. It would be easy to love and get along with people who like the same music I do, remember all my favorite TV shows and movies, share my outlook on life, and are concerned about the same things as I am. It's more difficult to love people from other generations, people with a very provincial way of looking at things, and, people with whom, at least initially, I may not have much in common. Yet learning to love is one of the most important things I can do. According to 1 Corinthians 13, if I don't have love, I don't have anything. I can be the best CEO the congregation ever had, but if I have not love, I am nothing. I can become the number one church-growth pastor in the country, but if I don't have love, I've gained nothing. Faith, hope, and love. These three—not my programs, not my goals, not my dreams and desires—remain. And the greatest of these is love.

What is love? It's putting other's needs, concerns, and reputations ahead of our own (Matthew 25:31–46; Romans 12:10; Philippians 2:1–4). It's treating others the way I want to be treated, thinking of others the way I want to be thought of, giving other people the same breaks I want them to give me (Matthew 22:34–40). It's making the first move toward people who may initially be unlovable (Romans 5:6–8; 1 John 4:9–10). It's sympathizing, empathizing, and walking with people through life's ups and downs (Romans 12:15). It's being nice to people who mistreat you (Romans 12:14). It's trying to get along with everybody as much as you can (Romans 12:16, 18). In short, it's much like small-church ministry. Learning how to live life as a small-church pastor is actually making me fit for the kingdom of God!

The Beauty of Obscurity

The universal church of Jesus Christ doesn't take much notice of small-church pastors. Sometimes we get the feeling that the work we do isn't all that important. In *Christianity Today* I can read about missionaries who were martyred for the faith, theologians who are working with their Roman Catholic counterparts to promote a new spirit of ecumenism, lobbyists who are witnessing to Washington's movers and shakers, a dedicated woman who single-handedly started an inner city mission, and so on.

What did I do last week? Well, I prayed for a little boy's lost cat, visited a couple of people in the hospital, prepared a Bible Study for ten people, led worship, and preached a sermon. Sometimes my small church seems very small indeed. And the pastor who stands behind the pulpit in the small church must also, of logical necessity, be very small. Sometimes I want to be *big!* I want articles to be written about *me!* I want *my* picture in the

paper. At the very least, I'd like the church-at-large to acknowledge that I exist.

Nevertheless, maybe it's better not to be noticed. Fame and
fortune carry with them temptations I don't want to face. Man's
original sin—pride—can easily rear its ugly head when voices
are singing your praises.

The small-church ministry keeps me humble. In fact, it may be
the very instrument that God is using to do so. After all, if the apostle Paul is any indication, God goes out of his way to make his servants humble. In 2 Corinthians 12, Paul talks of being taken up into
heaven and hearing "inexpressible things, things that man is not per-
mitted to tell." But then he says in verse 7, "To keep me from becoming conceited because of these surpassingly great revelations, there
was given me a thorn in my flesh, a messenger of Satan, to torment
me." From Martin Luther down to Billy Graham, many of God's
great leaders have had their own "thorns in the flesh," health concerns and other problems that kept them from thinking too much of
themselves and made them think even more about Jesus.

If, at times, being "stranded" in a forgotten part of God's kingdom is a "thorn in my flesh," it's a relatively painless one. In fact,
it's often quite pleasant. I shudder to think what God could use to
humble me. As more than one speaker has pointed out, when
Paul visited an area, the people didn't give him the keys to the
city. Instead, they showed him the inside of their jail!

Burdens or Blessings?

Our God delights in turning curses into blessings. He took a
young man who had been betrayed by his family, sold into slavery, falsely accused of rape, tucked away in an Egyptian prison,
and used him to save the chosen people. Later, Joseph said to
those who had betrayed him, "You intended to harm me, but God
intended it for good to accomplish what is now being done, the
saving of many lives" (Genesis 50:20). Centuries later, God used
a man, falsely accused of a crime and publicly executed in a
humiliating, tortuous manner, to save the whole world. The Bible
says, "For the message of the cross is foolishness to those who are

perishing, but to us who are being saved it is the power of God" (1 Corinthians 1:18).

Are there some burdens in your ministry that God wants to turn into blessings? What in your life seems like foolishness when it is actually the power of God? A lot depends on how you look at things. How does God want you to view your small-church ministry? Does he want you to see the young woman with the hat or the ugly crone? Which one does he see when he looks at the picture?

FOUR

We're Not in Kansas Anymore

Like the man in the mental ward who asserts that he's really James Bond on a mission for Her Majesty, or "Delta Dawn" in the country-and-western song who believes the "man of low degree" who violated her is coming back to take her to "his mansion in the sky," the small-churchaholic has a hard time accepting reality. Instead of cheerfully and energetically immersing oneself in the ministry God has given and making the most of it for him, the small-churchaholic spends an inordinate amount of time wishing that he or she was somewhere else. We come to believe that we won't be really happy and fulfilled until that magical day when the heavens finally smile on us and we're transported to our dream assignment.

When a patient refuses to accept reality and chooses to live in a fantasy world instead, there's only one cure—and it's not pretty. In this chapter I am going to have to administer shock therapy to you. I know it's going to hurt and I'm sorry about that. But I'm going to have to state reality as bluntly as I possibly can, without a lot of sugar coating. Trust me. It's the only way to get you to see your world as it really is; and that's the first step toward learning how to deal with it.

Brace yourself now—I'm turning up the juice.

Shock #1—You're Not in a Large Church

You're in a congregation that is not as focused on ministering to the world as they are on ministering to themselves. "Are all the shut-ins visited?" "Is everybody happy with what's going on in the church?" "How can we get our inactives to start coming back again?" "Can we raise enough money to repaint the steeple this year?" These are the questions the small church asks. They don't ask, "How can we reach our town for Jesus?" They aren't concerned with choosing a target group (Baby Boomers, Baby Busters, Generation Xers, Single Parents, etc.) and trying to meet its "felt needs." Cooperating with other congregations in order to present a stronger, more unified Christian witness is not high on their list of priorities. Reaching out to the poor in the community through social action is something the government's supposed to do—"we have our hands full taking care of our own."

You're in a congregation that concentrates on preserving the traditions of the past. They see no need to make five- and-ten-year plans for the church or to "cast a vision" for the church's future. They know exactly what the church's future is going to look like. Every September, Rally Day will kick off the Sunday school year. In October, there will be the annual Harvest Dinner. November will see the Thanksgiving Service. In December, there will be a congregational meeting and a Christmas Eve Candlelight Service. And on it goes. Woe betide anyone who attempts to change the sacred schedule!

You're in a congregation ruled by leaders you didn't choose. You don't have a paid staff to do your bidding. The power people in your church are the ones who have been there the longest, or who give the most money, or who have seemingly always done certain jobs, or who are the most popular. They are not people you have trained. They do not necessarily share your vision. They may not have even been formally elected to any position by the congregation, but everyone defers to them just the same.

You're in a congregation that feels threatened by outsiders. They are not interested in making their services more seeker-sensitive. "The seekers don't really belong here anyway if they can't understand and adapt to our ways." If too many new people start attending, "it just doesn't feel like the same church anymore." Your congregation isn't really looking to follow your lead—after all, you, as the pastor, are the ultimate outsider. They feel it is their job to ride herd over you and all of your wild ideas. While you're trying to turn them into the kind of church you'd want to attend, they are working to make you into the same kind of pastor that they've always had.

These are the general characteristics of the small church. By listing these, I don't want to give you the impression that small churches can never change or deepen in their desire to serve God. It's just that change agents, like yourself, must find ways to work within the existing culture and not try to work against it. One definition of insanity is "to do exactly the same thing in exactly the same way over and over again while each time expecting to get a different result." Many small-churchaholics move from small congregation to small congregation trying to implement megachurch strategies and always being shocked and saddened that their ministries fall apart. What's that say about our sanity? We've got to start implementing strategies that are designed with the small church in mind.[1]

Shock #2—You're in a Church That Is Unlikely Ever to see Rapid, Dramatic, Numerical Growth

Ninety percent of the churches in America have fewer than 200 members.[2] This means that large churches and megachurches are definitely in the minority! They may get all the press, but there is a "silent majority" of Christians out there who will never know what it's like to attend one. Statistically speaking, the chances that you will end up pastoring or leading a church that "really takes off" are very slim indeed.

The megachurch is the exception, not the rule. It grows when there is an unusual combination of timing, location, high-powered clergy, exceptional lay involvement, favorable economic conditions, and special outpourings of the Holy Spirit. Larry Gilbert of Church Growth Institute says:

> Taking the 102-member church and turning it into a 5,000-member church requires extraordinary leadership. That cannot be our definition of success. Bill Hull, director of church

ministries for the Evangelical Free Church in America, has written, "Those who pastor the megachurches are usually individuals who have charisma and special gifts. Even though they like to promise pastors of small struggling churches, 'If I can do it, you can too,' it's just not true for most of those who attend church-growth seminars and conferences."

We need to help pastors turn a 102-member church into a 112-member church. If this consistent growth, however small, were to happen in thousands of churches, it would revolutionize the body of Christ.[3]

I wonder if you caught the "aftershock" or "shock no. 2A" in the above quote. If not, let me turn up the juice a little more so you can really feel it. Many of those ideas in your church-growth conference notebook? They won't work for you! Let me hit the button again. They won't work for you! Why not? Well, look in the mirror and get ready for "shock no. 2B": *You're not Bill Hybels or John Maxwell or James Kennedy or Chuck Swindoll!*[4] Stop driving yourself crazy trying to be.

There are other reasons why the ideas won't work for you. You may be in an area of the country that is resistant to church growth. I minister in the North East. Whether it's because we are in the "Burnt-Over District," or people are still rebelling against the strict Puritanism of centuries ago, or New Englanders have a stubborn, independent streak which rebels against people trying to tell them what to believe, or so many are nominally Catholic or Protestant and feel they already have a connection to a church (even though they never attend), the fact is that growing a congregation up here is a slow, arduous process. (Just think of all the church-growth experts who are ministering in the North East. Why, there's . . . uh . . . er . . . and then, of course, who can forget . . . um . . .)

A young woman from our area moved to Atlanta and was shocked at the way the expressway was jammed on Sunday mornings. She was even more shocked when she heard the reason: "Everybody's going to church!" Up here, you could play a game of football on the highway at ten o'clock Sunday morning.

Actually, the people around here do spend Sunday mornings playing football, and baseball, and soccer. The youth sports teams and town leagues all play on Sunday mornings. There's always one Sunday in the spring when my church will be missing one-quarter to one-half of its members. It's the day of the registration and kick-off picnic for Little League. Craft shows, trade fairs, art exhibits, horse shows, etc. also regularly begin during church hours on Sunday. Everyone and every organization rushes to take advantage of "the one day when people are free of other commitments." Church just doesn't count. Or, to put it more accurately, there aren't enough Christians to count.

Our choir director was saddened to see that our local public school scheduled a children's concert on Ash Wednesday. When she told the powers-that-be that this would conflict with church services, they replied, "But so few people attend the service anymore that there really isn't a problem." And the powers-that-be were right. Maybe you, like me, live in a part of the country where your spiritual seed is falling on hard soil indeed. Maybe you, too, minister in an area where social pressure for and support of religious activities and institutions is almost nonexistent. The American West, for example, has significantly lower rates of church membership than even the East.[5] Should you reasonably expect to be able to build the next Crystal Cathedral there?

In some parts of the country, the population is declining (for instance, in the Great Plains states). Maybe it's because a major employer is downsizing, moving, or going out of business. Maybe it's because the taxes are too high. Perhaps the products which once fueled the area's economy are no longer in demand. Technology may have made some goods and services obsolete. There could have been an environmental disaster. Ancestors may not have planned for the future. Whatever the reason, congregations will remain small in these areas because you can't grow a church without people. I know this is an obvious truth, but it's often overlooked in "Rah Rah" church-growth literature.

Maybe your congregation has what C. Peter Wagner calls "a terminal disease." Perhaps your church neighborhood has changed dramatically over the years, so that the people who commute to the worship service no longer live near the church. Instead, the inhabitants of the area are of a different culture, race, language, or social status. Your church has "ethnikitis." If there are no young people moving into your area, there will be little chance that a church can grow in any of the three ways churches add members—babies born, memberships transferred, or new conversions occurring. Your church is dying of "old age."[6]

Preparing churches to close their doors, working people through the grief process, selling the congregation's property, and seeing if a different type of congregation could use your building are the priorities of a pastor ministering in a terminally ill church. You should no more waste your time on growth strategies than you would attempt to teach a ninety-year-old man on life support to roller blade.

Not that God can't and won't cause some congregations to grow in very hostile environments and in the most unlikely circumstances. He can and will. But not always. And it seems, not often. We small-churchaholics set ourselves up for bitter disappointment when we expect that God will do something he never promised to do. A young pastor moved into a small town to take over a small charismatic church. I commented to him that the town needed the gospel. In that small community there were at least three bars. "Give me two years," he said, drawing himself up to his full height, "and I'll close them down." Well, now it's been six years. I was back visiting the area and saw that the bars were still alive and well and the church was still small. I wonder if the pastor is still dreaming his impossible dreams.

To sum up, as Loren B. Mead writes:

> The case I am making is that dozens, hundreds, even thousands of congregations have not had that experience of explosive growth, and probably won't; they *may* (emphasis his), but it's not likely. Most pastors now working in congregations and most congregational leaders will live their lives without experiencing any dramatic changes in church membership. With a few exceptions, that has always been true of

church growth. We celebrate the exceptions (as in some areas of East Africa today, for example), and we should work hard to be such an exception, but the chances are that we will have to work all our life without that experience. If our faith cannot handle that, we are in trouble.[7]

Get it?
Got it?
Good.

Shock #3—You're Not in Seminary or Bible College Anymore

In school, you are the center of attention. The professors are being paid to answer your questions and to make sure you are receiving a proper education. You get to spend hours bouncing your theological theories and observations off your peers. When you do your field education or Clinical Pastoral Education, you write papers and attend focus groups in order to answer these questions: "How did I feel during this experience? If I was uncomfortable, why? What could I have done better? What further training do I need? Did I get enough support from my co-workers? What is my relationship with my co-workers? How has this experience helped in my spiritual formation? Has it deepened my understanding of God and the ministry? What unanswered concerns still remain for me?"

In ministry, though, the focus is on the congregation. Are their needs being met? Are their concerns being listened to? How can they become all they are capable in the Lord of being, as individuals and as a church? What ministries does the congregation do well? In what areas does it need work? Are the people growing in their understanding of the faith? How did a certain tragedy (death, fire, tornado, etc.) affect their lives?

The small-churchaholic wants to focus on "Me! Me!" all the time. Do I like what's going on here? Are my ideas being well-received? How is my faith doing? How do I feel about the way the church is treating me? Does everybody like me?

During the 1996 presidential campaign, Ross Perot kept saying, "This is not about me, see. It's about the future of the American people." In the small-church ministry, I have to make it a point to tell myself over and over, "This is not about me, see. This is about the eternal destiny of this group of people." Actually, Ross wasn't the one who said it first. Jesus Christ did:

> "If anyone would come after me, he must deny himself and take up his cross and follow me. For whoever wants to save his life will lose it, but whoever loses his life for me will find it" (Matthew 16:24–25).

> "Whoever wants to become great among you must be your servant, and whoever wants to be first must be slave of all. For even the Son of Man did not come to be served, but to serve, and to give his life as a ransom for many" (Mark 10:43–45).

> "Now that I, your Lord and Teacher, have washed your feet, you also should wash one another's feet. I have set you an example that you should do as I have done for you" (John 13:14–15).

If I can't learn to give up myself in service to others, I can't be a true follower of Jesus Christ. Being a small-churchaholic is then the least of my problems.

In school, you were engaged in a quest for truth. Your mission was to soak up the Bible, fill the gaps in your theology, contemplate the plan of God unfolding in church history, and seek the Lord and the counsel of godly friends in order to determine your place in that plan. You got to touch base and interact with the best and brightest Christian thinkers (whether in person or through their writings). Large chunks of your time were spent reading, reflecting, and wrestling with faith and doubt.

In the ministry, however, you are often too busy to find time to pursue truth. You're engaged in a quest, all right, but it's the quest to find a more efficient way to run a small volunteer organization, not a quest to uncover the meaning of life.

I know that many today are advocating that pastors abandon the day-to-day business of running the church in favor of becoming spiritual directors. The spiritual director spends his or her time much the way it was spent in school—reading good books, boning up on biblical studies, meditating and reflecting—with large amounts of prayer and fasting thrown in for good measure. This way, when the members of your congregation have problems they will be coming to find help from someone who has been calm and quiet before the Lord. The spiritual director will have such a depth of understanding and such a passionate love for God, that he or she will easily be able to point the seeker to Jesus. Crises in the church won't rock the spiritual director, because he or she has been with Jesus.

Well, all I have to say is, "Nice work if you can get it!" For better or worse, this is not the small church's view of the pastor. Maybe they can and should change their view, but like any change in the small church, this will only happen over a long period of time. My congregation isn't just paying me to prepare sermons and Bible studies. After all, they reason, how long can that take (how little they know)? They're certainly not paying me to sit around thinking holy thoughts all day long. They are paying me to attend committee meetings, to be up to date on what various groups in the church are doing, to listen to Mrs. Johnson's complaint (yet again) that younger women don't want to join the ladies' fellowship, to let repairmen into the building, to provide guidance when the annual budget is drafted, to help out with fund-raising, and to find volunteers for the various tasks that have to be done at church. While I may wish to be only a spiritual director, I am, in fact, also an administrator and the nerve center of my congregation's communication network.

Is this really so wrong? Most workers in the small church have to wear more than one hat. Why not the pastor? One woman in the small church may have to teach Sunday school, sing in the choir, organize the craft show, and serve as a deacon. The same man in the small church has to be the treasurer, do "handy man" repairs, head up the missions committee, and serve as elder. Why shouldn't the pastor have to be spiritual director, administrator, nerve center, and manager? If I am counting on my people to do multiple jobs, can I myself do any less?

Several young pastors were complaining that they never got to do ministry (make long-range plans for the future, start new programs, spend hours in prayer, search the Scriptures for God's word to the congregation, etc.) because of all the interruptions. The older pastors in the group laughed. One said, "Friends, interruptions *are* the ministry." And he was right. Not only is your congregation expecting and paying you to be interrupted, but also, as you deal with the interruptions you get a chance to interact with your people and touch them beyond the one hour on Sunday morning. You, as pastor, remind them of God's holy presence in their day-to-day lives. They, as a congregation, pull you out of your ivory tower, making you face the real world, making you more human.

Let's face it. If the only way one can grow in the Lord is by retreating for hours on end into the study, then what hope is there for the guy in your congregation who has to work a grueling eight to five job Monday through Friday, with a hectic commute on both ends, and overtime on Saturday? To say nothing of the mother of young children whose needs never end all through each and every day and night. What kind of message do I send him or her if I maintain that, for my spiritual health, I need to take a three hour walk in the woods every day? I'm unconsciously telling my people that there's no hope for them to ever grow in the Lord—unless they become pastors.

In school, all things come to an end. Terms end, projects get completed and handed in, requirements are met, exams are taken, and the bell rings dismissing class. You can head for home over semester break with no pressures hanging over you. All your work has been finished.

The small-churchaholic goes through ministry waiting for the bell to ring and it never does. There's always someone else going into the hospital. Next Sunday's sermon has to be researched. There are more committee meetings to chair. You need to call that couple that missed their counseling appointment and see how they are doing. What about looking up the answer to the Sunday school teacher's question? Somebody else has a relative going through a crisis and wants the person put on the prayer chain. Meeting the needs of people and attending to a dynamic organization like the church are ongoing tasks. Rare are the times that I've been able to leave for vacation feeling as though I'm all done. There are always several things I've left up in the air.

The problem is not so much that I've left things unfinished as it is that I feel *guilty* about it. The problem is not so much the ongoing nature of ministry as it is that I resent it and keep expecting it to be different.

A friend and I have come to the conclusion that all pastors need to learn to be "Christian Buddhists." In Buddhism, one is taught that it is not one's circumstances that are evil, it is one's desire to change those circumstances that causes all the problems. If one could just learn to accept life as it comes and purge away wishes and desires, one could be at peace. If pastors could only give up the desire for a time when no sick or hurting people need to be visited, no decisions will have to be made, no "fires" will have to be put out, and nobody will call during a Knicks' game, they could be at peace.

Actually, one doesn't need to turn to eastern systems of thought to learn this same lesson. All you have to do is open your Bible. In Philippians 4:11–13, Paul talks about dealing with diverse situations. Rather than moaning about them or wishing they would change, he says, "I have learned to be content whatever the circumstances. . . . I [know] the secret of being content in any and every situation, whether well fed or hungry, whether living in plenty or in want. I can do everything through him who gives me strength."

Everything except be a small-church pastor? Of course not!

In school, you are one of many. A student interacting with other students. You have the privilege and luxury of being surrounded by like-minded people—others who share your passion for debating doctrine, for diagnosing the health of the church today, for reaching a lost world with the gospel of Jesus Christ.

In ministry, as a pastor, you stand out among the many as one who is different. You interact with others who don't know what your life is like. Rarely can you find anyone who shares your passions. Their passions are their careers, their hobbies, their extended families, their traditions, their children, their schools, their sports, and their community. And these are the things they love to talk about.

Aristotle defined friendship as one soul sharing two bodies.[8] The pastor often feels as if part of his or her soul is missing. Small-churchaholics go around searching for the missing piece, and set themselves up for disappointment after disappointment as each relationship fails to live up to expectations.

But can it really be any other way? The pastor is supposed to be the spiritual leader of the congregation. A leader is the man or woman who is out in front. You are supposed to be ahead of those you minister to in your understanding of the Bible and theology. You are supposed to be dissatisfied with the state of your congregation, or else how or why would you ever try to spur them on to growth? You're supposed to be bringing an outside perspective— God's—into the world of your congregation. You've got the training, the time, and the resources to be able to do this. Your people don't. If your people do ever get to the point of fully understanding you and relating to you, it may be time for you to move on! Your effectiveness as a leader may be diminished.

"It's lonely at the top," is an old cliché. A phrase only gets to be an old cliché if it's repeated over and over. It's repeated over and over because it's true. A certain amount of loneliness comes with the job. Not that there aren't ways for you to find friends and supporters and to deal with loneliness. We'll look at some of them later in the book. For now, realize that you are always going to be slightly out of step with your congregation. But this is a good thing. God can use your "alien-ness" to get the attention of a sleeping church.

Shock #4—You're in the Army Now!

To start this section off, I've asked Bishop George S. Pardoned, veteran of many evangelistic campaigns to address us. Now, I know his methods are a little unorthodox, but they get results. Yes, this is the same Bishop Pardoned who spotted a pastor looking down in the dumps at a seminar.

"What's the matter with you, son?" Pardoned asked.

"I'm stressed out, sir."

"Stressed out? Stressed out?" Pardoned screamed. "Boy, you're nothing but a coward!" Whereupon the Bishop slapped the pastor across the face.

So, let's all smile really, really wide and welcome Bishop George S. Pardoned:

"At ease. Smoke 'em if you got 'em, unless you belong to a denomination that doesn't let you. Listen up! I've been asked to talk to you about small-churchaholism. Now, what kind of New Age, psychobabble, self-justifying term is that? Can you say *sin?* Harumph! I'm sick to death of all you mamma's boys whining whenever a phone call interrupts your prayer time. In other parts of the world, believers are getting their entire lives interrupted— by bullets!

"So, you have to go to a Sunday school meeting tonight but you'd rather stay home and watch a movie? How'd you like to go to jail instead? Too soft, that's the problem. Didn't they teach you in those fancy seminaries that it's called spiritual *warfare* (Ephesians 6:10–18)? Did you bother to read your recruitment brochure? Our Commander-In-Chief said, 'In this world you will have trouble' (John 16:33). 'If they persecuted me, they will persecute you also' (John 15:20). You thought life was going to be just one big praise-worship concert, didn't you? You thought the only wound you'd ever receive would be when you'd pull a muscle lifting *The Complete Works of Jonathan Edwards* off your bookshelf.

"What about General Paul saying, 'I bear on my body the marks of Jesus' (Galatians 6:17)? Didn't he talk about the internal pressures he felt over his concern for his churches (2 Corinthians 11:28–29)? He instructed Lieutenant Timothy, 'Endure hardship with us like a good soldier of Christ Jesus' (2 Timothy 2:3). You're like characters in those so-called comedy movies about our blessed armed services that *Hollyweird* puts out. You know—the recruit telling the barber how he wants his hair done or the one who asks his boot camp sergeant if he can have weekends off. You act like everything that happens in the Lord's service is a complete surprise to you!

"Doesn't the Bible depict church fights (Acts 15:36–40; 1 Corinthians 1:10–12; 3:1–3; Philippians 4:2)? Doesn't it tell you that congregations sometimes reject their leaders (2 Corinthians 10:1–11; Galatians 4:12–16)? Shouldn't you have been forewarned that this is what the pastor faces at times?

"Yes, there will be pain. (Speaking of that, if you try to put this book down before I'm done, you'll find out what real pain is.) But there will also be glorious victories. You see, we're not just called to suffer for Christ, we're called to make Satan and his minions suffer through the power of Christ. Stop moaning and get out there and inflict some pain yourselves! Kick some demonic butt! Dismissed!"

Thank you, Bishop. You gave small-churchahol ... I mean, sinners ... er, whatever ... something to think about. We do spend far too much time complaining about the pain that is inherent in the life we've chosen.

Another old saying, full of truth, is, "War is hell." The object of warfare is to hurt the enemy badly enough so that he will be forced to surrender. At the same time, the enemy is doing his best to hurt you badly enough so that you will be forced to surrender. There's nothing pretty about the process at all. Yet the small-church-aholic still wants to win the world for Christ without engaging in any messy battles himself or herself. It simply can't be done.

I try to get to a health club two or three times a week to use the exercise machines. While I enjoy the energy, health, strength, and improved appearance exercise gives me, there are times when I don't enjoy the exercise itself. In order to build new muscle tissue, you have to first break down the old. And it hurts. But as the weightlifters are fond of saying, "No pain, no gain." This should be every pastor's motto, hanging up on the wall of every pastor's study. "No pain, no gain." You will never lead your church to spiritual health, renewed vitality, increased spiritual strength, and improved ability to attract nonbelievers without gritting your teeth and pushing through pain somewhere along the way.

To keep me going through the pain, I turn to stories about men and women dealing with the challenges of battle. Try watching war movies and westerns and ask yourself this question: What does this tell me about the Christian life in general and about the pastorate in particular? I recommend the following films:

Twelve O'Clock High—Gregory Peck as a small-churchaholic in denial.

The Caine Mutiny—How back-biting, mistrust, and conspiracy drive leaders nuts.

Patton—The inspiration for our beloved bishop. 'Nuff said.

Sands of Iwo Jima—The few, the proud, the Duke.

Glory—Men are granted the dignity of fighting and dying for what they believe.

The Searchers—John Wayne relentlessly searches for his kidnapped niece.

The Outlaw Josie Wales—In the aftermath of a brutal war, Clint Eastwood learns about forgiveness, acceptance, and family.

The Magnificent Seven—Yul Brynner and company put themselves on the line so that others can live secure, normal lives.

High Noon—Gary Cooper as the unappreciated, unsupported savior of the town.

Rio Bravo—John Wayne and a small, unlikely band of defenders take on the bad guys.

I gain inspiration from *Star Trek*, too. I'm a science-fiction fan anyway, but it's also the military aspects of the programs that intrigue me. I appreciate Kirk's daring "risk it all" attitude in order to save his ship, Picard upholding his moral code when the easier thing to do would be to blow the aliens to bits, Sisko leading a group that isn't really sure it wants him there, and Janeway making the best of a bad situation and constantly assuring everyone that they will reach their goal. One of my favorite lines comes from *Star Trek: Voyager*. Ensign Kim is commenting on how weird their latest adventure was. Captain Janeway replies, "Mr. Kim, we're Starfleet officers. Weird is part of the job." There are many times I have to remind myself, "You're an officer in God's army. Weird is part of the job."

As a leader in God's army, I must learn to delegate. No general ever won a war on his own. He depends on his troops, information gatherers, strategists, officers, the weathermen, the munitions manufacturers, etc. The small-churchaholic, though, sets out to win the war single-handedly. It seems easier that way. You don't have to constantly check up on volunteers who are off doing who-knows-what and ruining your plans. But it's not biblical. Ephesians 4 reminds us that its our job "to prepare God's people for works of service" (v. 12) and that the church "grows and builds itself up in love, as each part does its work" (v. 16). According to the Bible, it's totally impossible for you to grow a church on your own.

There's really no excuse for not getting more of your congregation involved in ministry. You shouldn't wear yourself down to a frazzle trying to do everything yourself. But even more seriously, you must not stifle the growth of the body of Christ and hinder its victories. I once heard about women in a foreign land who had their feet bound up at a very early age. As they grew up, their feet remained twisted and crippled so that even when their feet were finally unbound, they could never walk normally again.

This, of course, was the point. Women were possessions and had to be kept from running off. Just as a man would fence in his animals, so he "fenced in" his women. Many pastors "fence in" their congregations by refusing to let their people stretch their muscles. Maybe they do it because deep down inside they don't want their congregations to run off on them, trying things on their own, coming up with new ways to serve God. Pastors want to be needed, noticed, and appreciated. They want to feel indispensable. But when the pastor finally leaves a congregation and the shackles are removed, the people won't know how to stand on their own. Ministries in pastorless small churches often grind to a halt or go right down the tubes. Instead of setting your people up for a fall later on, why not unshackle them now and teach them how to stand, walk, and run on their own? Why not leave a congregation healthier than when you found it?

Are there obstacles to doing so? So what? A good soldier finds a way to overcome obstacles.

You may say, "Nobody ever responds to my pleas for help." Personalize those pleas. Don't just make announcements from the pulpit and put blurbs in the bulletin and the newsletter. Most people won't respond to, "We're looking for someone to help run the sound system. Anybody interested contact the pastor." People respond better to a personal invitation. "Phil, I appreciate the fact that you faithfully attend church every week. And you seem to have a good ear for music. We've got a little problem now and I'm wondering if you could help us out. We need someone dependable to help run the sound system. We're willing to train you. It's not that difficult. How about it? Is this something you'd be interested in doing?"

You may be saying, "I'd love to enlist new workers, but our long-time members have a stranglehold on all the key positions and jobs in the church." Well, challenge your long-time members to prepare the church for the future. Small-church people are always talking about keeping the church going for "our kids" (even if the likelihood is that "our kids" are all going to move away). Getting new people involved and educated in the ways of the congregation is one concrete thing that can be done for the next generation. Also, ask the long-time members to help train new workers. Say, "We need someone who knows the way around to show them the ropes." People want to feel important. They don't want to feel as though they are being put on the shelf in favor of younger blood. By making long-term members part of the training process, you give them the sense of significance and value they need.

Speaking of the training process, you may be asking, "How would I find the time and the energy to educate a bunch of volunteers?" Training doesn't need to consist of the pastor writing a lot of extra printed material and holding special classes. You can train people by simply inviting them along as you do the tasks you hope to turn over to them later. For example, elders learn to do visitation by accompanying the pastor and then talking with him or her about what happened on the visit later. This is the way Jesus trained his disciples. He took them along with him as life and ministry happened and then reflected on the events with them.

You may be saying, "My people expect me to have a finger in every pie." Yes, well, your people probably have a lot of wrong and sinful attitudes. As pastor, is it your responsibility to correct them or just leave them stranded in their muck and mire? Constantly refer people to the "experts" in the congregation. "George knows more about computers than I do. Why don't we give him a call and see if he can figure out why the bulletin won't print?" "Fred's quite a handyman. Let's get his input on whether or not the door needs to be replaced." "Mary has a real heart for children's ministry. Maybe she's got some ideas about getting the youth more involved." "Sue's our bookkeeper. If you want facts and figures on how the church is spending its money, contact her."

Direct the attention away from yourself and put the spotlight on others. Eventually, people will stop calling you about certain things and go right to the "experts." Sometimes projects are going on in my church that I, the pastor, know nothing about. I jokingly say, "Don't ask me. I just work here."

Just as you are not the only worker in the church, so also you are not the only officer in the church. Small-churchaholics get bent out of shape whenever their boards question their plans. You need to stop thinking of yourself as the commander-in-chief. When you attend a board meeting, you aren't there to issue commands. You are there to work on problems alongside of others. Think of the fellowship hall, lounge, or Sunday school classroom where your board meets as being the Pentagon. One person does not run the Pentagon. It is like the ultimate government "think tank." Your board should be a "think tank" for Christ. You and your board members are military leaders who have been called by The (true) Commander-In-Chief, Jesus Christ, to plot out the best way to carry out his campaign. You and the other leaders *together* will discuss manpower, financial resources, strategies and tactics, intelligence reports, timing, goals, casualty reports, etc.

Board members usually aren't the only officers in the small church, either. Sunday school teachers, choir directors, respected and revered long-time members, even your secretary may be just as high in rank in the eyes of the congregation as you are (or even higher!). You will be expected to confer with others, plan with them, cooperate with them. You will not be expected to order them around. If you do, you'll be court-martialed in no time. Not that you have to obey all their orders, either. But you do have to seriously consider their advice and work out compromises with them, if necessary.

It's likely you will also receive input from officers in the universal church as well—seminary professors, conference speakers, seminar leaders, authors, older pastors, etc. The thing you must remember is not to be intimidated by them. They are merely peers offering advice. They are not superiors who can give you orders. But this is the way the small-churchaholic often treats them. You go to a training session and return with a notebook crammed with good stuff—new evangelistic programs, notes on how to be a "take charge" leader, ways in which your worship facility needs to be remodeled if it's ever going to attract non-believers, a plan for starting cell groups, and "10 Reasons to Switch to Praise and Worship Music." You then proceed to carry out your ministry "by the book," knowing that if you just follow the orders of General Church Growth Superstar, your church will come alive and burst at the seams with new members. However, it rarely works out that way. The general cannot and does not know the particulars of your character and style, your congregation, or your territory. And so, his orders won't always fit. The Lord doesn't want our congregations run by remote control from long-distance leaders.

I'm not trying to run down the recognized "experts" in the Christian world. I have benefited and grown from much of their *advice*. For example, my ministry today wouldn't be what it is if I had been ignorant of Wagner's "Sociological Strangulation."[9] My congregation would have stopped growing and I wouldn't have the slightest idea why. But I take what the experts say *as advice*, not commandments. I evaluate it, adapt it if I can, and sometimes reject it. I treat the experts the same way I treat the officers who are working with me in the small church. They have some good ideas and some that just won't fly.

You may feel funny thinking this way at first. Who are you to go against General Superstar? I remember the total shock I felt, shortly after I was ordained, when one of my former seminary professors asked for my opinion at a presbytery meeting. He was treating me as his equal! He knew that the same Lord who had commissioned him, also commissioned me. And the same Lord who made General Superstar an officer, also made you an officer. General Superstar and you are serving on the Lord's staff together. Treat the superstars as your partners, not as your idols.

Sorry I had to be a little brutal in this chapter, but once you stop twitching from the shocks, I hope you will thank me for it. I know that reality hurts at times. But what alternative is there?

FIVE

Get a Life

A group of seminary students was invited to dine at the home of a famous evangelical thinker. Looking forward to an evening of stimulating discussion, the group planned questions and topics to bring up. However, as supper began, their hopes were quickly dashed to the ground when, after their first question, the host said, "Look, I have to do theology all day long. It's my job. At home, however, I want to talk baseball."

The students were stunned. They had been expecting "Table Talk" with a modern-day Luther; instead they wound up dining with a Nero Wolfe, who refused to discuss "business" away from the office. And maybe it was just disappointment talking, but afterwards, some of the group began to question the thinker's sincerity and commitment to the faith. After all, if one really loved Jesus, wouldn't one want to talk about him all the time? Shouldn't one be willing to part with anything in the world to serve Jesus? Doesn't "anything in the world" include major league baseball?

Actually, their famous host was closer to the spirit of Luther than the students knew. In order to ward off or cure spiritual depression, Luther would work in the garden or go down to the local tavern and listen to the music. Luther knew that you had to take a break from wrestling with "the great and important spiritual issues of the day" once in a while, or else you'd go nuts (or wind up as a small-churchaholic, which is practically the same thing).

I have a confession to make. I often find as much refreshment, rest, relief, and recharging in pursuing my hobbies as I do in having my quiet time. Organizing and indexing my comic book collection can leave me with as much a sense of well-being as reading a few Psalms. After playing a game of chess with my son, I can believe just as strongly that God is in charge and will take care of my problems as if I had just come from a time of prayer with my ministerial colleagues. Touring a museum, I can become just as convinced that God wants me to stay at my current church as if I had spent hours on my knees seeking his will. Yelling myself hoarse over a basketball game can set my mind at as much ease as if I had just spent an hour singing praise-worship songs.

Now, before you prepare to burn me at the stake as a heretic or dismiss me as being too carnal, let me say a few words in my defense. First, it's biblical to enjoy the good things in the world (Psalm 104:14–15; 1 Timothy 4:3–5). Second, I'm not claiming that hobbies can or should ever replace spiritual disciplines; rather, they often have the same immediate effect on me as the spiritual disciplines. Why? Because spiritual disciplines and hobbies alike take me temporarily away from whatever problems are demanding my attention. They remind me that the universe is bigger than my small congregation and whatever happens to be going on in it at the time. The spiritual disciplines put me in touch with the larger universe of God, his power, and his plans. My hobbies put me in touch with the larger universe of humankind and the creativity, gifts, and variety that God has given us.

And *small*-churchaholics need to be exposed to *The Big*. Otherwise, you won't be able to see the forest because all the trees will keep getting in your way. Rather than getting an overall feel for what God wants to do through your ministry, you'll fixate on problem people and situations. Instead of getting a feel for what life is all about, you'll start to believe that it consists solely of what goes on within the walls of tiny First Church. And First Church can seem overwhelmingly big if you have nothing larger to measure it against.[1]

The Problem of Perspective

Perspective is a real problem. As a small-churchaholic, you engage in a lot of "stinking thinking"—thoughts that seem so right but are completely wrong, thoughts that seem "holy," but are actually crippling you and destroying your life. And some of the stinkiest thinking of all is that your happiness and fulfillment depend on things that are relatively small in the overall scheme of the universe: whatever your tiny congregation does or doesn't do; whether you can or can't get along with a few cantankerous individuals; whether or not you can solve the problems of the handful of counselees who come to you.

At first glance, it seems right and proper for you to endlessly obsess on these little things. After all, you're a pastor. You have been called to this small group, and you take your calling and identity very seriously. You want to be a faithful servant of Jesus Christ. You want to shepherd, plan, teach, and pray—all of which require thought, and lots of it. Also, many small churches live life on the edge. If a couple of people leave the congregation, the church may not be able to staff its Sunday school or pay its bills. Therefore, it seems as if it's absolutely necessary for everybody to be kept happy all the time. And isn't this your job as the pastor, to make sure the church retains enough members to survive?

As the pastor, you are the center of the small church's world. There will always be groups and individuals demanding your attention. Pastoring a small church is much like being the parent of young children. Because you are the center of their world, they are always yelling, "Mommy, look at what I can do!" "Daddy, I got a boo-boo!" "I'm hungry." "I'm scared." "Johnny's not sharing his toys with me." "I have to go to the bathroom!" And many parents of small children find that even when they go out for an evening without the kids, all they can talk about is their offspring. They are, of necessity, so used to paying constant attention to the children that even when they don't have to, their minds can think of little else. The same thing happens to pastors, right? Endlessly concentrating on your congregation is normal for the pastor. It's not a sign of serious problems.

Or is it? Tragically, some couples who have talked exclusively about their children for years find that they no longer have anything in common once the kids have grown up and moved on. If all

you think about are the people and concerns of your small congregation, there may come a day when you sadly realize that you
literally can't think about anything else. There will seemingly be
no "you" left apart from "you" as "the pastor."

Also, if absolutely everybody else in the congregation has to be
happy before you can be happy, then resign yourself to a life of
anxiety and feelings of helplessness. You've turned control of your
life over to others. Who knows what they will do with it? And you
won't be able to do a thing to stop them.

Finally, is it going to do your congregation any good if you burn
out? What will become of your calling if you end up in a mental
ward or selling cars somewhere?

Therefore, from time to time you must focus your mind on
something else. Don't be like some pastors I know who have as
their hobby reading books from their pastoral libraries. (Can you
pronounce *workaholic?*)

Find a hobby that can instantly engage you each time you take
it up—either because it demands your attention (like sewing or
carpentry or learning musical instruments), or because it instantly
transports you to another world (like reading or watching movies),
or because it forces your body into action, dragging your brain
along (like sports). If you can't "get into it" in a hurry, then it's probably not the hobby for you. If you have to work at it, you won't.
You'll claim that you're too tired from church work, then immediately go back to thinking about the church. I know. I'm a small-
churchaholic, too, remember?

Pursue a hobby that you enjoy. This may seem obvious, but I
know the way many small-churchaholics' minds work. Some will
say, "The book I'm reading says I have to choose a hobby. Let's see—
okay, I pick birdwatching. Now I've got to go out in some field and
waste time waiting for the stupid little things to flitter by. I suppose
I've got to buy some binoculars and, of course, a washable hat in
case the unthinkable should happen. I've got to do all this because
somehow it's supposed to be good for me. Well, we'll just see. I dare
this to be good for me. In fact, I double dare it!" And, lo and behold,
a week or two later they will go back to making the congregation

their sole preoccupation. "Yeah, I tried that hobby stuff, but it didn't work. My calling is to be a pastor, not an ornithologist."

Choose a hobby that fits your budget. Believe me, I know how tight finances are for small-church pastors. Maybe you can't collect paintings, but you can go for long walks in the woods or visit an art museum. Maybe you can't afford carpentry tools, but you could learn to whittle. Maybe you don't have the money for formal music lessons, but you could buy a "teach yourself" book on the harmonica or recorder.

You may have to try out a few hobbies before you find the one that's right for you. After all, you probably didn't start out in life preaching and leading a church. (If you did, then you belong in an "Adult Children of Religious Fanatics" recovery group, not reading a book about small-churchaholics.) Somewhere down the road, you tried out the ministerial role, found it fit you, and that you were good at it. Experiment with different hobbies. Find the ones that fit you. Do research. We pastors love to do that anyhow, don't we? Visit hobby shops or newsstands or your local library. Surf the internet and check out hobby chat rooms. Come to think of it, researching hobbies can in itself be a hobby. It can take your mind off your day-to-day responsibilities and keep you occupied.

Hobbies: Friend or Foe?

Some pastors worry that they will become so occupied with their hobbies that their ministries will suffer. This is a real danger. We small-churchaholics have addictive personalities and we can just as easily fixate on collecting baseball cards as we can on the problems of our congregations (particularly if we're in problem congregations). A few years back when I was serving a very difficult church, my hobby of comic book collecting began slowly starting to take over my life. It became nearly all I thought about. I counted the days until the next new shipment would arrive at my local comic shop. I spent way too much money on back issues. I got too caught up in storylines, writing letters to the editors, and worrying about the characters as though they were real people. One day my wife lovingly, but firmly, told me, "Steve, your hobby has become your god." Although I didn't want to admit it at first, I knew she was right. Finally, I loaded up my collection, drove to the dump, and, feeling like I was cutting out my heart, threw every last book away. Now, I'm collecting again, but it's under control. (I don't dress up as Batman and climb up in the bell tower to brood over the city.) And I trust my wife to tell me when I'm going dangerously overboard again. Trusted friends and ministry partners (see next chapter) can help you pursue a hobby while minimizing the risk.

It's worth taking the risk, not only for your own sanity, but also because your hobbies may actually enhance your effectiveness as a pastor. After all, the people you are ministering to don't spend all their time thinking theological thoughts or mapping out strategies for community outreach. How will you be able to develop relationships *with* them (and in the small church everything rises and falls on relationships) if you can't relate *to* them, nor they to you? In my congregation, I have people who discuss *Star Trek* with me (one man installed a moving field of stars as a screen saver on my office computer because he knew I'd get a kick out of it) and people who share my frustrations with the New York Knicks (a championship ring is always so near, yet so far away). Sharing hobbies goes a long way toward helping to make me "one of the gang."

My hobbies help me communicate spiritual truth to my people. Seeking to explain how it can be that Christ's death affects us, I talked about the Chicago Bulls winning their fourth NBA Championship. When it happened, I found myself yelling, "We did it! We won!" I'm sure Michael Jordan and Scottie Pippen would look at me and say, "What do you mean, 'we', Steve? Were you with us hustling up and down that court?" Well, no, but because the Bulls were the Eastern Conference champs, and therefore my representatives, their victory was my victory. Their joy was my joy. Their accomplishment was my accomplishment. And when they celebrated, I celebrated. I tied this in with Christ's death. He represented humankind on the cross. When he died to sin, we died to sin. When he rose again and claimed victory, it was our victory over the grave. His ascension to the Father's right hand (his "victory parade") was our celebration and now we can tap into his joy.

Once in a sermon, I compared Jesus Christ to Columbo, the TV detective. It's easy for people to dismiss the bumbling lieutenant in the crumpled raincoat as being no threat to their plans and schemes. But, during the last half hour of every episode, they suddenly come to the shocking realization that he sees them for who they are, knows every detail of their crime, and is about to expose them to the world. It's easy for people to dismiss a carpenter who lived two thousand years ago as being totally irrelevant to their lives today. When they think about a god, they picture Eastern deities, or a nameless force, or even themselves, not a beaten, bleeding man on a cross. Yet, when the last act is played out, they will discover that he is the one who sees them for exactly what they are, who knows every detail of their lives and hearts, and who is about to expose them to the Father. I urged the congregation to recognize Jesus for who he is now, rather than waiting for the last act.

My parishioners comment on the fact that they can actually understand my sermons (the idea of understanding and not just sitting through a weekly twenty minute talk by the pastor is novel to some of them!). They say that they appreciate my illustrations. In my case, my hobbies not only help me get a life, but they also help many others find life.

Small-churchaholic, come down out of your ivory tower and get out on the greens, into a bowling alley, or onto the slopes. Leave your commentaries for the movie theater or the fabric store every once in a while. You and your people will be glad you did.

SIX

Who Was That Masked Man?

One of my favorite TV shows when I was a boy was *The Lone Ranger*. I wanted to be the famous masked man and I loved to act out his adventures. But I discovered something quite ironic. Despite the character's name, you really can't play the Lone Ranger all by yourself. You've got to get someone, your sister or a friend, to be Tonto (as long as they can pronounce "Kemo Sabe"). For the Lone Ranger to be without Tonto is simply unthinkable. In fact, in the Ranger's original story, Tonto saves his life after he is wounded by Butch Cavendish's Hole-in-the-Wall gang. So, if it weren't for Tonto, there wouldn't even be a Lone Ranger.

As a small-churchaholic, you've got to understand that no matter what you want to call yourself—the pastor, the shepherd, the preacher, the leader, the reverend, the spiritual director—if you are going to survive, you're going to need some faithful sidekicks. For you to try to go it alone without some Tontos should be unthinkable.

It certainly is to God. In his Word, we clearly see that team ministry is supposed to be the rule, not the exception. Aaron and Hur held Moses' hands up when he grew tired (Exodus 17:12). Jonathan helped David find strength in the Lord (1 Samuel 23:16). Jesus sent out his followers two by two (Luke 10:1). Paul traveled with missionary companions (Acts 13:2; 15:40–41; 16:10). Ecclesiastes 4:9–12 teaches us that, "Two are better than one, because they have a good return for their work: If one falls down, his friend can help him up. But pity the man who falls and has no one to help him up! Also, if two lie down together, they will keep warm. But how can one keep warm alone? Though one may be overpowered, two can defend themselves. A cord of three strands is not quickly broken."

Think of the great leaders throughout church history. Where would Luther have been without Melanchthon? Calvin would never have gone to Geneva except for the exhortations of Farel. John Wesley began his open-air preaching at the urging of George Whitefield. Could Billy Graham put on a crusade without the work of his evangelistic association?

If God and church history be for it, who are we to be against it? Yet it's often hard for the small-churchaholic to open up to his or her peers, to expose any wounds so that a Tonto might arise and tend to them. Small-churchaholics often wrestle with feelings of guilt, shame, and a poor self-image. Such a person does not easily admit his or her weaknesses to others.

The Very Lonely Ranger

Early in my career, I never participated in ministerial fellowship groups. This was partly because I felt that pastors were supposed to be strong and have no need for "touchy feely" encounter groups. But mostly, I think, it was out of fear. As a small-churchaholic, I had a deep need for everyone to like me. If people knew about the struggles going on in my heart and mind, would they reject me? So I kept to myself. It didn't take long for the Lone Ranger to become the *Very Lonely* Ranger. And loneliness drives a man to desperate acts—even finally sharing!

The book you now hold in your hands is largely the result of my opening up to other pastors. As I began to share my struggles, yes, some looked at me as though I was from Mars, but the majority of pastors said, "We're in exactly the same boat!" I was encouraged by seeing that I was not alone. Not only that, but I also saw that others seemed to be helped as I shared insights I had learned from ministry. And I certainly learned a lot from the others. I discovered tremendous value in sharing with my peers (now I'm even doing it in print!). And I believe you will, too. At the very least you'll be able to say, "There are others like me! I'm not crazy!"

How do you go about gathering others like you together? Start by issuing invitations to the other pastors in your area to get together regularly for lunch (brown-bagging it is okay) or coffee and dessert to "talk shop." You don't have to stick only to pastors in your own denomination. If you're ministering in a remote rural area, there may not be many pastors nearby who share your convictions or polity. It really doesn't matter. You'll find that being a pastor automatically gives you all the common ground with other ministers that you need. Although I am a "conservative evangelical," I have learned much about people and church politics from "liberal" pastors. Although I am theologically in the Reformed camp, I gained a new understanding of, and appreciation for, Methodism when three Arminian pastors explained to me Wesley's belief in "prevenient grace."

It's good to have some sort of agenda for your gathering. It can be as simple as always checking in for a few minutes with each person, finding out how his or her life and ministry are going, and then finally ending with a group prayer for concerns raised. It can be even more structured. You could all decide to study a book on pastoral ministry, or some aspect of it, together. Before each meeting, everyone would read the next chapter. Members of the group would alternately be assigned to be leaders, preparing a few questions to guide the discussion.

If you don't have an agenda, you run the risk of spending the meeting talking about golf, computers, politics, or the latest episode of *Home Improvement*. Then pastors will start to drop out, labeling the whole thing as "a waste of time." (I'd be one of the first to quit.) Having an agenda does not lock you into a rigid structure. I have never known a fellowship group to tell a pastor on the verge of a nervous breakdown, "We don't have time to listen to you today; we've got to cover chapter three." The group is always free to set aside or change the agenda as circumstances warrant. But an agenda ensures that the meeting will always be about something.

It's also wise to have a predetermined time to wrap things up. Pastors are busy (or like to think of themselves as being busy, at least). They are more apt to come to a meeting set from noon to 1:30 than they are to come to an open-ended gabfest. The quitting time doesn't have to be set in stone. Someone sharing a story doesn't need to quit in the middle when the bell rings. But participants should be free to quietly exit, if need be, when the time is up without feeling awkward or having to make a lot of excuses.

How often should you meet? That's up to the group. Some ministerial fellowships meet weekly, others monthly. My current group meets the first and third Tuesdays of every month. Just make sure that everyone can usually attend. There has to be some measure of commitment and accountability here. Nothing will kill the meetings like, "I was just too busy to make it this week," or "I needed the time to catch up on some work." When a member doesn't attend, make sure you give him or her a phone call just to say, "We missed you," and to find out how things are going. We small-churchaholics are creatures of bad habits, and it's easy to fall into the habit of skipping meetings, even ones that are important for your soul.

Keeping in Touch—One Way or Another

If you live in a really isolated spot, make use of modern technology to keep relationships going with pastors living elsewhere. There's this wonderful newfangled invention called the horseless carriage. Get yourself one. While I was serving one church, my pastoral friends and I lived at least an hour and a half away from each other. We found a restaurant that was about 45 minutes from everybody and drove there once a month for lunch. How were we able to take this kind of time away from our congregations? We told our people the truth. "I've got an important minister's meeting to attend." Nobody will argue with you if you tell them you've got a meeting. Meetings are sacred, don't you know?

One pastor I know finds refreshment sending E-mail back and forth to his friends. I often take a tape recorder along with me as I run errands or drive to pastoral calls. I make "talking letters" to some of my seminary classmates, sharing my joys, frustrations, problems, and observations. They, in turn, record over them (after listening to them, I hope) and send them back to me. I find I do enough writing as a pastor and an author that I have no desire to put pen to paper and write letters (if you do have such a desire, more power to you!). But I still stay in touch and it helps me make use of the "wasted" time on the road. Of course, if you are independently wealthy, you can always just pick up the phone. But on an average small-church pastor's salary, I wouldn't recommend doing so very often.

The Church Member You Live With

However you do it, the important thing is to stay in contact and dialogue with those the Lord has given to you for encouragement, understanding, challenge, wisdom, prayer support, and love. This includes some who are right under your nose, but are often overlooked: your spouse and the leadership of your congregation. Some pastors feel that it's not right to share too much with them, but I believe those pastors are dead wrong and are ignoring valuable members of the body of Christ.

"You shouldn't burden your spouse with the problems of the church. Don't you want him or her to be able to go to church and enjoy worshiping the Lord without worrying about who's saying what about whom? Remember that you are the one whom the Lord has called and equipped to be the pastor, not your spouse." See? I know all the arguments. I even used to believe them myself until two things happened: I got married and I pastored a small church.

I hadn't realized how true the saying "the two will become one flesh" really was until I got married. I can't hide anything from my wife, nor she from me. She can definitely tell when something's bothering me. My moods, attitudes, and secret thoughts affect her. Because we are "one" and because she wants to be "a helper suitable for me," she wants to be there for me, to provide a sympathetic listening ear so I can talk things out. And she knows me better than anyone else on the face of the earth. She can, therefore, give me insight that *nobody else* can give. Why would I want to hurt myself and my ministry by cutting myself off from my best counselor?

And why would I want to hurt *her*? I once talked with the wife of a pastor who was having a hard time in his church. "I only know he's angry all the time," she said. "I don't know why. And I don't know what to do about it." She felt helpless, frustrated, and left out of the problems that were dominating her husband's life. She wasn't "relieved that she was being spared the burdens." She felt that she and her husband were drifting apart. A woman in that position can easily imagine the worst about people in the church, or even that she herself is the reason her husband is so upset. Is it really a kindness to hide the truth from her? Particularly when everybody else in the congregation already knows it?

It's almost impossible to keep a secret in a small church. Early in my ministry, I used to try to hide from Deborah what went on at elders' and deacons' meetings, only to find out later that their wives knew all about it, as did their friends. Why should my wife be the last to know? People in the congregation assumed that she already knew about everything anyway. They would call her up and begin talking with her about "the news." Also, because we've always been in small churches, people call me at home. If I'm not available, they will relay their messages (many times in gory detail) to Deb.

It didn't help matters any when we once lived in a small apartment. Of course my wife was going to overhear what I was saying to others! Even if she went into the bedroom and shut the door, she was still only fifteen feet away. Maybe in a large church, the pastor can leave the office and come home for the evening. In the small church, the home and office are often interchangeable and our spouses are going to be part of our work, like it or not.

Many small churches still have definite roles in mind for the pastor's wife. Deb would find people complaining to her about the women's group or the Sunday school or the nursery and she wondered why. Then it dawned on her—as the pastor's wife she was somehow expected to seize control of these programs and fix them to everybody's satisfaction. She would often be drawn into church politics against her will.

Short of blindfolding the small-church pastor's spouse and filling his or her ears with wax, I can't think of any way to keep him or her from discovering things they "shouldn't." Why not hear it from you instead of through the grapevine?

Not that I share everything with Deborah. There are times when I return from a counseling appointment and just say, "Those people are having a tough time and it's getting to me. Pray for me." No confidences are broken, but I still give her the opportunity to express her care for me. At other times I'm thinking about a problem in the church and I realize, "She doesn't really need to know about this in order to understand me or the congregation." Or, as I'm beginning to pontificate, she might stop me herself and say, "I really don't need to hear this. I just want to know how you're feeling about it now." Sometimes I'll come back from a meeting and just tell her, "It was typical small-church stuff. Nothing to worry your head about." But if something is eating me up inside or is threatening our future in this field of ministry, she needs to know about it. And more importantly, I need her to know about it.

Making Partners of Leaders

I need my leaders to know when something is amiss, too. The New Testament makes it very clear that the local church is to be shepherded by a team, not by one individual (Acts 20:17, 28–31; Philippians 1:1; 1 Thessalonians 5:12–13; 1 Timothy 3:1–13; Titus 1:5–9; Hebrews 13:17; James 5:14). In the small church, the chances are that these shepherds have either been in the congregation or lived in the area longer than I have. They probably know more about any trouble-making individuals than I do. They can put church struggles into historical perspective. They have background information that I'm lacking. I need the wisdom and insight that they can bring to the challenges our church faces.

Not that I tell them absolutely everything either. Church board meetings aren't supposed to turn into therapy sessions for the pastor. But if there is something going on with me that is effecting my ministry, I'll share it. For example, I don't run to my elders every time I receive criticism about something. However, in one congregation, when an individual's constant criticism was wearing me down and wearing me out, I went to them and we dealt with the matter together.

From time to time, too, I will feel the need to get my elders' insight into a counseling situation or my deacons involved in helping a counselee with material needs. Remember, your leaders often have known your counselees longer than you have. They may know some things you don't. I ask the counselee's permission first before I share anything. I let my boards know that the counselee agreed so they won't think I've broken a confidence or that they are hearing "forbidden," confidential knowledge.

At the instigation of one of the elders, Cobblestone started a policy of having a different elder each month take me out to lunch and ask me how I'm doing. Is there anything he or she can be praying about? What do I think is going well in the church? What am I concerned about? What are my dreams for the church's future? And I return the favor by asking each of them the same kinds of questions. It's a release valve for all of us and, more importantly, it makes sure we're always on the same page.

Every February, we are required by the denomination to conduct a pastoral review. The board of elders and I separately answer a set of questions that probe my job performance, the health of the church in general, and our goals for the coming year. Then the board and I get together to share our answers. Even though I always agonize over writing my part of the thing and dread the meeting, we inevitably wind up laughing with each other and saying, "Well, there are no real surprises here." As one elder reminds us, "In a healthy relationship, there shouldn't be." Do all you can to minimize surprises in your relationships with your leaders.

Spending Time with God

You should try hard to enjoy a true partnership in ministry with your layleaders, your spouse, and your pastoral colleagues. However, there's one other important, indeed essential, person that you need to have as a partner if your ministry is going to be fruitful and you're going to keep your sanity: God Himself. Often he seems to be the hardest one of all to share with.

Maybe you are like me. For some reason I find it very difficult to spend a lot of time with the Lord in prayer about the church or my struggles in it. Not that I think that prayer is unimportant. Far from it! I know that the ministry is utterly impossible without the power of God behind it. "Unless the Lord builds the house, its builders labor in vain" (Psalm 127:1). I believe that, "You do not have, because you do not ask God" (James 4:2). I can testify that it's only prayer that gets me through the Sunday services. I've seen miraculous answers to prayer—from healings, to church rabble rousers suddenly calming down and becoming agreeable, to vacation plans for this harried pastor suddenly falling into place, to very tangible signs when I needed them that God loved me. When people ask me why Cobblestone is growing, I can truthfully answer, "Because my wife and children and my parents pray about it." When my daughter Abigail was three and a half years old, there weren't any kids in her age group for a Sunday school class. She decided to pray for more children and that fall a class started up with eight enrolled in it!

It's not that I don't pray, but my prayers tend to be short, on-the-spot, "arrow prayers" rather than three-hour sessions of wrestling with the Almighty on my knees. I've asked myself why: Why can I spend hours talking to other pastors and my wife about my concerns, but only minutes talking to God? I think the answer partly has to do with my small-churchaholism.

As a small-churchaholic, I tend to think that my efforts are never good enough. When it comes to prayer, I get easily intimidated when I read pastors advocating that all ministers spend at least one hour a day, if not more in concentrated prayer. When I try to pray, my mind wanders, the phone rings, my eye catches some work on my desk that needs to be finished, etc. Before I know it, I'm no longer in prayer. Then I have to apologize to the Lord for blowing it and start over. Then I blow it again. And so it goes. My "hour in prayer" might boil down to fifteen minutes, if I'm lucky. Then the guilt sets in. Could I not "keep watch one hour?" Compared to the *real* pastors, I don't stack up.[1] What does God think of my puny attempts at prayer? Wouldn't he rather go listen to James Kennedy or Dr. Dobson or somebody? It doesn't take me long before I give up trying to pray prolonged prayers altogether.

I also start to envy the pastors who *can* spend hours in the divine throne room. And when I start to realize why many of them can, the green-eyed monster bites me even harder. Many of them have a secretary to screen calls, shoo away unwanted visitors, and ensure they have uninterrupted, quality time with the Lord. I do not. Some of those pastors regularly take a day away from work to go on personal mini-retreats, getting alone with the Lord in a motel room or a conference center. I don't have the finances, nor the "time-off" (for that's what the congregation would surely see it as), to do so. As for finding a quiet spot to get alone with God, my office is in the house along with two high-energy, home-schooled children. It doesn't take long before the small-churchaholic's "poor pitiful me" attitude takes over. And then I don't want to talk to God because he's the one who put me in a small church to begin with.

Another reason I find it hard to spend hours in prayer is that God actually answers my "arrow prayers." He is gracious and loving enough to hear me and take action, even if I'm not as eloquent or as attentive when I come to him as some are. Small-churchaholic, take heart! If God blesses my meager efforts, he can certainly bless yours! Don't stay away from the Lord because you can't pray like Reverend Superspiritual. Don't neglect the power, guidance, help, and comfort that are yours for the asking. "If any of you lacks wisdom, he should ask God, who gives generously to all without finding fault, and it will be given to him" (James 1:5).

Maybe in my struggle with prayer, the Lord is teaching me an essential lesson that I must learn if I'm going to recover from small-churchaholism—it's okay to be myself (see Chapter 10). Maybe "arrow prayers" fit my personality, temperament, and way of thinking more than prayer marathons do. And maybe that's okay with God.

When people shake my hand Sunday morning and give me prayer requests, it's easy for me to pray silently for them then and there and say quick prayers whenever I think of them during the week or pass their houses on the way to the supermarket. If, however, I sit down in my office with a long list of prayer requests to get through, the task seems overwhelming. And my prayers seem much less sincere. Then, I'm praying prayers in order to check them off of my mental list of things to do, not because I'm remembering and loving my people. And rather than communing with God, I'm just reciting a laundry list of needs to him.

Also, I'm a person who hates repetition. I even find it hard to put the chapters of this book down on paper because once I have outlined in my mind what I want to say, the project seems finished to me. It seems redundant to write it down, as if I'm covering old ground. I want with every fiber of my being to move on to something else. Unfortunately, Zondervan can't publish a book full of blank pages with the introduction, "Don't worry, it's all in Steve's head." So I force myself to write.

After I've talked with others about my problems and the state of my congregation, I see no need to talk it over with God. In my mind, it's already been "talked out." I don't really see the need to do it again. If I do sit down to pray, something inside my head asks, "Didn't God already hear you say all this when you met with Pastor Goodbuddy?" Often my prayer becomes, "Lord, you know what's going on and you know I can't handle this alone. I need your help. Either give me the insight and power I need to deal with the situation or change it with a miracle. I really need to see your hand here. And if I've done something to cause or exasperate the situation, I'm sorry. Show me how I need to change. In Jesus' name, Amen." While I may repeat this short prayer many times during that day and over the course of the next several days, I hardly think I can be classified as a "prayer warrior." Yet, God answers my prayers.

Maybe God isn't calling me to be a "prayer warrior," after all. In fact, maybe many of the burdens I carry around as a small-church-aholic haven't been placed on me by God, but rather by well-meaning (and not so well-meaning) people and by evangelical and pietist traditions. We'll talk more about this during the next chapter and in chapter 10. For now, though, realize that God is waiting for you to come to him in prayer, however simple or halting your prayers may be.

Remember, too, that when you pray God wants to hear from *you*. Don't feel the need to imitate or compare yourself with someone else. I know God is not a cosmic "Mister Rogers," but when it comes to prayer, at least, it's true that "God loves you just the way you are."[2] Need proof? Then consider these "proof texts":

The apostles said to the Lord, "Increase our faith!" He replied, "If you have faith as small as a mustard seed, you can say to this mulberry tree, 'Be uprooted and planted in the sea,' and it will obey you" (Luke 17:5–6).

"Which of you, if his son asks for bread, will give him a stone? Or if he asks for a fish, will give him a snake? If you, then, though you are evil, know how to give good gifts to your children, how much more will your Father in heaven give good gifts to those who ask him!" (Matthew 7:9–11).

"And when you pray, do not keep on babbling like pagans, for they think they will be heard because of their many words. Do not be like them, for your Father knows what you need before you ask him" (Matthew 6:7–8).

Then they called on the name of Baal from morning till noon. "O Baal, answer us!" they shouted. But there was no response; no one answered. And they danced around the altar they had made. At noon Elijah began to taunt them. "Shout louder!" he said. "Surely he is a god! Perhaps he is deep in thought, or busy, or traveling. Maybe he is sleeping and must be awakened." So they shouted louder and slashed themselves with swords and spears, as was their custom until their blood flowed. . . .

At the time of sacrifice, the prophet Elijah stepped forward and prayed: "O LORD, God of Abraham, Issac and

Israel, let it be known today that you are God in Israel and that I am your servant and have done all these things at your command. Answer me, O LORD, answer me, so these people will know that you, O LORD, are God, and that you are turning their hearts back again." Then the fire of the LORD fell and burned up the sacrifice, the wood, the stones and soil, and also licked up the water in the trench (1 Kings 18:26–28, 36–38).

God wants to be your partner. What are you waiting for? "Hi-Yo, Silver, awaaaaaaaay!"

SEVEN

Pastor Yourself

To the many hats you already wear as a small-church pastor, prepare to add one more. Nancy J. Foltz writes, "Ministry in the small church usually means that you are your own secretary, custodian, and *spiritual leader*."[1] And she's right. In a small church you must be your own pastor. You will have to take your own spiritual temperature, determine what your soul needs in order to be healthy, and make provisions to be fed from God's Word.

In a larger church, you would probably be a member of the pastoral staff. In many such churches, the staff meets several mornings a week for Bible study and prayer. The other pastors in the church would pastor you, and you, in turn, would pastor them. The small-church pastor, in contrast, faces a regular morning meeting with just "Me, Myself, and I." In a larger church, when a staff member meets you at the water cooler, he or she may ask, "How's your walk with the Lord?" In the small church, you ask yourself, "Where did I put the phone number of that visitor we had last Sunday?" After you return from a conference or seminar while serving a larger church, you'll be *asked*, "What did you learn? How can we put it into practice here? How did you do in the battle against temptation while you were on the road?" Upon returning home in the small church, you'll be *told*, "Mrs. Jones had another one of her breakdowns last Friday and she became frantic when she found out you weren't here!"

If you even get to go to conferences and seminars. Many small congregations cannot afford to send their pastors and the pastors, on their salaries, cannot pay for these things themselves. And you may be ministering in an out-of-the-way small town so that traveling a great distance to a conference would be impractical.

So, in the small church, if you are to keep growing spiritually and professionally, you're going to have to be a self-starter. If you won't take care of you, no one else will.[2]

How does one keep growing spiritually? The traditional evangelical answer has been, "Make sure you have your daily devotions (or quiet time)." As a small-church pastor, this has never worked for me. I don't have a secretary to hold all calls while I commune with the Lord. People in a small church really don't understand it if they know the pastor is at home or in the office and yet he or she won't answer the phone. Members of your small church consider you part of the family. Don't you want to talk to your family? Don't you want to be immediately informed whenever there is a family crisis? Where were you when the family needed you? And being there for the family means that you can throw any ideas you may have about keeping a consistent personal schedule out the window. You are going to get calls late at night when a family member has just been rushed to the hospital. Can you come right away? You're going to receive calls early in the morning from family members who need a word of counsel, encouragement, or prayer before they can face the day.

Your meals will often be interrupted by the ringing of the phone or a knocking at your door. You'll have to attend a lot of committee meetings or hear reports on the meetings you couldn't attend (not during any regularly scheduled appointments, but whenever chairpersons happen to think about it and pick up the telephone or drop by). I have tried to carve out a consistent time for devotions. I've tried having them at morning, noon, or at night. Invariably, I do okay for a little while but then I have a couple of hectic weeks and my daily devotions go the way of all flesh. What's a small-church pastor to do?

How about making the most of the times you are able to spend reading God's Word and meditating on his truth instead of feeling guilty about all the times you can't? This is hard for small-church-aholics because we are addicted to feeling guilty. And we've been told that "all good, growing, evangelical Christians must spend at least fifteen, if not thirty, or sixty, or ninety minutes each day in personal Bible study. God has given you twenty-four hours, can't you give him back twenty minutes? You take the time to eat each day, don't you? Shouldn't you also take the time to feed your soul? What kind of believer are you if you don't desire the pure milk of the Word? How will you ever be able to move on to meat?"

But while immersing yourself in Scripture so that your thoughts and character may become more godly is certainly biblical, I have yet to find one text that commands me to have daily devotions or else be eternally damned, or relegated to second-class status in God's kingdom. In fact, some historical perspective may be helpful here. Let's remember that believers living in Bible times didn't even have their own personal copies of Scripture (much less printed daily devotional guides)! How then did they ever grow in the faith? By attending the public worship meetings, listening to the Word preached and taught, and meditating on what they remembered during the week. We can grow by doing the same.

As a pastor, I'm in the enviable position of never having to miss a Bible study or a worship service because of job conflicts. I've learned to view these meetings as opportunities for growth. Just as the busy members of my Thursday night study tell me that they really need it to get them through their week, so I've come to see I need it to get through mine. Just as members of my congregation tell me that they are thinking about what I'm saying in my sermons and trying to apply it to their lives and the life of our church, so I try to let my messages speak to me. After all, they aren't really "my messages," but God's messages to his people. And I'm one of his people.

I get into trouble when I try to artificially separate time for just me from time spent doing my job—leading and teaching God's people. Because I'm a pastor, I get to spend more time in the Bible or meditating on Scripture than most people do. Even during a hectic week, I still have at least one Bible study, a children's message, and a sermon to prepare.[3] The problem is that I often feel as though I have to cram my daily devotions in on top of all that. Why should I? Why do I really need to find a way to spend an extra thirty minutes a day doing what I've already been doing all week? Why weary and burden myself with this additional, and superfluous, chore?

If done with a prayerful and meditative attitude, your exegesis and lesson and sermon prep can serve as your devotions.[4] While you're asking, "Lord, what do you want to say to the congregation through this passage," why not also ask, "Lord, what do you want to say to *me* through this passage?" If your study should lead you down a path that is unrelated to the immediate needs of your congregation, go ahead and indulge yourself, exploring it for a little while. After all, we pastors have to grab for the gusto while we can. If in the middle of looking up the derivation of a verb, you are suddenly convicted of a sin, take a moment to confess it to the Lord. If, as you're reading a commentary, you receive an answer to a personal problem, take a moment to stop and praise the Lord. If the passage you're working on reminds you of a hymn or praise-worship song, why not take a few minutes to sing it to the Lord?

Instead of keeping a spiritual journal, why not let your sermons and Bible studies serve as your journal? They are the record of what God has been showing you. If you preach and teach what the Lord is showing you, you'll preach and teach with enthusiasm and heart-felt conviction. In fact, don't be afraid to preach sermon series on topics or books of the Bible that interest you. After all, as I said earlier, in the small church you are your own pastor. I'm sure that many times members in your congregation have said to you, "Pastor, I think we need a few sermons on thus-and-so. I'd really like it if you'd preach through the Book of Whatever—it's my favorite." So, don't be afraid to say to yourself once in a while, "Pastor, I'd like you to spend some time on Fill-in-the-Blank." If the subject excites you, chances are that it will interest your congregation, too. If it speaks to your deepest spiritual needs, chances are that it will speak to theirs' also. After all, we are all just sinful, struggling members of the human race. Also, if you've been pastoring the same small church for quite some time, you probably have begun to think, act, and maybe even look, like the others around you. This always happens in families. Their concerns have become your concerns and vice versa.

Along with changing (or expanding) your definition of devotions, you may need to change your definition of meditating on God's Word. As a pastor, you may find yourself doing it often, even when you're not aware of it. I can finish making one of my tapes to a friend (see last chapter) and feel that something spiritual has taken place. And indeed it has, for I don't just tell my friend all about my trials and church struggles, I also try to reflect on them theologically. "Where is God's hand in all this? How can I discern his will? What is he saying to me and to the congregation? Are there any biblical parallels to what I'm going through? What would Paul do in my situation?" Once again, I find I'm having my quiet time without having a *scheduled* quiet time. As a small-churchaholic, you spend an awful lot of time thinking about everything going on in your church and doing spiritual navel gazing. Not all of that is "stinking thinking." Some of it, or maybe even most of it, is theological and biblical in nature. Can it be that instead of destroying your spiritual life, the small-church ministry is actually God's goad to spur you on to growth?

The Best-Laid Plans

The small-church ministry has taught me humility. Despite my best-laid plans and (to my mind) flawlessly executed presentations, things often don't end up going the way I thought they would. Maybe I can't control the destiny of this congregation. Maybe it's God, not me, who's really in control after all. I continually wrestle with trusting him and not leaning on my own understanding, or being crippled over my worry about the future. I'm learning what it means for a leader to also be a servant, because the nature of my job places me at the disposal of others. I'm learning to persevere in love, to stay committed to a group of believers through many ups and downs even when there are seemingly more attractive groups elsewhere.

I've learned how to hang onto the Lord through hard and hectic times and I've felt just how tightly he hangs onto me. Just a few weeks ago, a friend of mine in the church died at a young age of cancer. I was with the family in her hospital room when the doctors, fearing that she was brain dead already, turned off the machine that had been breathing for her and let her pass away. At the same time, a thirteen-year-old boy from our congregation was suffering unexpected complications after heart surgery. To make matters worse, the elders and I were also in the midst of trying to decide how to handle a very delicate discipline problem in the church. And the deadline for my book kept creeping closer and closer. Though I shed tears daily and felt close to collapsing many times, the Lord was with me. He gave me strength, guidance, and love and enabled me to minister to others at a time when I would have rather received ministry.

So, let's see: learning humility, trying to trust God for the future, persevering in love, persevering in faith, experiencing firsthand God's persevering grace—all of this sounds like spiritual growth to me. And it's happened for the most part while I was doing ministry, not while I was sequestered away from it having devotions. If you think about your own situation, I'm sure that you can come up with specific examples of personal spiritual growth that have happened to you as you were pastoring your congregation. In fact, the small-churchaholic in me wants to order you to put this book down right now and come up with at least five. I'll be on pins and needles until you do. And if you don't, I'll be personally crushed. However, instead I'll just *suggest* that sometime you do so and then take the time to thank the Lord for placing you in a position that forces you to grow up.

But what about those times in the ministry when your growth seems to have halted, when you can't detect much, if any, personal progress? When personal or church problems are overwhelming you to the extent that you can't even see God any more, what do you do then?

As your own pastor, you really only have one option. You've got to schedule a counseling appointment with yourself. Sit yourself down in your office (or if you also have a degree in psychology or psychiatry you can lay yourself down on the couch), tell yourself what's bothering you, and then advise yourself on how to fix it.

If you're uncomfortable with the idea of talking to yourself and it all seems just a tad too schizophrenic for you, consider the biblical precedent. In Psalm 42 and 43, the author writes, "Why are you downcast, O my soul? Why so disturbed within me? Put your hope in God, for I will yet praise him, my Savior and my God."

For me, the ultimate experience in talking to myself came during the time I was making the final changes on my first book. I had entered that altered state of consciousness that comes from working long hours reading the same thing over and over again. Several times over the course of the job, I found myself for a few seconds wanting to call my wife to say, "Hey, Deborah, wait until you read this new author! I find myself agreeing with everything he says! It's like he's lived my life. He knows me so well." And then, I would grin sheepishly (to myself, of course), and realize what had been going on. It must have something to do with the Zen of book writing. Anyway, I have benefited from going back and re-reading my first book and the manuscript for this one. Just today a friend was telling me that the Lord had been dealing with him about leaving the results of his ministerial labors up to God, and I was reminded of the points I'll be making in chapter 12. I went over them again in my head and they helped lift me out of the dark blue funk that I had fallen into the morning after the meeting of our local denominational judicatory.

On another occasion, I tried to get my board to institute two worship services on Sunday mornings. Even as I was making my pitch, I knew I was violating all my own principles for bringing about change in a small church. Sure enough, the idea was defeated. Being a small-churchaholic, I started to get discouraged and to look down on the congregation. But then I told myself, "You dope! You knew better, but you let impatience and enthusiasm run away with you. The smart thing to do is wait awhile and bring the matter up again, this time following the advice of that Bierly fellow." I did, and we now have two services.

Ask Your Self

You may not have bound volumes of your thoughts to refer to, but you can still give yourself your best advice when things get rocky. Ask yourself what you would tell a parishioner or a colleague who was going through the same types of things you are. Tell yourself the same things. Would you give him or her a homework assignment to do? Give yourself the same assignment.

— "Self, it seems to me that you need to read First and Second Timothy again to gain some perspective and encouragement with regards to the ministry."

— "Self, it's been too long since you've had a date with your spouse. Get your calendars and yourselves together fast!"

— "Self, think back on some of the other dark times in your life. Remember that the Lord brought you out of them. He will do the same again. In fact, Self, what kinds of things did he use to snap you out of it in the past? Do you think maybe he could use these same things again? How about exposing yourself to those things and seeing what might happen?"

— "Self, each night for a week, right before bed, think of two things you can thank God for. Just say a simple prayer of thanksgiving."

— "Self, you need to find a way to get more fellowship with other Christians."

— "Self, find one task in your mountain of work that you can complete tomorrow and feel good about finishing. Set your alarm, get out of bed, and get it done. Then give yourself some kind of reward—a special food treat, a movie, a walk in the park, etc."

Pastoral counseling books are full of these kinds of things. Why not search through some in order to find an answer to your problem? You would take the time to do that for other people. Why not take the time to do it for yourself?

As you seek out resources to help you grow, don't neglect pop-ular Christian books, videos, and music. I know that, as pastors, we can sometimes exhibit a kind of cultural snobbery toward material that's capturing the attention of our laypeople. "Of course they think it's good. They don't know any better. I, on the other hand, with my theological training . . ." And, to be honest, there is an awful lot of "Jesus junk" out there. But there are some nuggets of pure gold as well. Years ago my mother recommended that I read *A Step Further* by Joni Eareckson and Steve Estes. She said it made a lot of good points about God and suffering. My first thoughts were, "Yeah, right. Isn't Joni just a young woman who experienced a tragedy and now travels around the country giving a hearts-and-flowers testimony? On the other hand, I am a Reli-gion/Philosophy major. I've read C. S. Lewis's *Problem Of Pain*. I've written a paper on the book of Job. I've debated the issues in classes, seminars, forums, and over countless lunch tables with my fellow students. What could Joni possibly have to say to me?" However, at my mother's gentle encouragement, I finally picked up the book. Whoa! I was knocked back on my heels by the depth of the insights I found there. I couldn't put it down as it chal-lenged, comforted, and confronted me. And it was easy to read! That's the beauty of popular books. You can pick one up when you're way too tired to wrestle with Barth, Calvin, Berkhof, or the latest critical commentary.

A question is often asked, "Who pastors the pastor?" Joni Eareckson Tada, Philip Yancey, Chuck Colson, Chuck Swindoll, J. I. Packer, John Stott, Elisabeth Elliot, Eugene Peterson, Ben Pat-terson, and others have been my pastors—authors who write sim-ple, but not simplistic, books; who deliver messages, not lectures; who stretch the soul without wearying the mind; whose popular-ity makes me believe that maybe, just maybe, there is hope for evangelicalism after all.

Some of my pastors have also been musicians—Larry Norman, Keith Green, Glad, Bob Dylan(!), Noel Paul Stookey, and others (including my wife). Their music has helped me worship God, find encouragement when I needed it, and meditate on the Lord's truth and the world (and how the two intersect). And through the magic of audio cassette, these pastors can minister to me while I'm in the shower, making lunch, driving in the car, or dozing off in my recliner.

Even material designed for another generation can be helpful to me. The other day, as I was feeling down, I heard my son playing some rap and alternative Christian rock on his cassette player— loud (the *only* way to appreciate rock 'n' roll). Now, I'm forty-two years old, at the age where I should be shaking my head at the young people and labeling their music, "Noise." However, I certainly recognized the Holy Spirit's power behind many of the selections and found my own spirits starting to lighten. Could it be that dc Talk, Geoff Moore, and johnny Q. public are my new pastors?

I've also been blessed by the ministries of Pastor Quigley and the members of his village, as well as the Reverends Larry the Tomato and Bob the Cucumber, not to mention Bishop Donut Man. If you don't recognize these names, you probably don't have young children around the house. They are all characters in kids' Christian videos. Watching them with my daughter can make me laugh and cry and, in general, make me feel that it's great to be a Christian. After my kids are grown, I'll have to come up with excuses to keep buying them. ("They are for the church library. Yeah—that's it—the library!")

Some authors and artists may be popular simply because they pander to the lowest common denominator or water down the truth to tickle the ears. Others, though, are popular because they speak to the universal human condition and the longings of the Christian heart. Instead of watering down the truth, they make it easily accessible. As a busy pastor, you need truth that is easily accessible. Don't ignore the tremendous sources for growth available to the "average Christian." It's just possible that the people in the pew know something you don't.

Practicing What We Preach

I need to say a word about integrity here. If I, as a pastor, can't find ways to grow spiritually because my job keeps me too busy, tired, stressed, and bummed out, what right do I have to preach to my people that they should be maturing in the Lord? In today's hectic world, they're just as busy as I am. The members of my congregation are involved in the public schools, the fire department, youth sports leagues, scouting, Love in the Name of Christ, Birthright, the hospital chaplaincy program, and Schenectady City Mission, as well as Cobblestone Church. Some are going to school for advanced degrees. A good number of them are caring for sick relatives. And most are two-career families on top of all this. Many confess that they can hardly remember whether they are coming or going at times.

If my job and lifestyle give me a "valid excuse" for not deepening in the faith, the members of my congregation have even more such "excuses." How dare I chastise them for their failure to do what I myself cannot? Physician, heal thyself! I need to take the log out of my own eye before I worry about the speck in my neighbors' eyes. I want to get to the point where I can honestly say to my people, "Imitate me, as I imitate Christ." I'm called to tell others, "I've found ways to grow. You can, too!" I'm not supposed to sigh, "So you want to become a mature Christian? Well, lots of luck to you. You'll need it."

Along with growing spiritually, you must also grow professionally. Small-churchaholics often wonder why they should bother sharpening their ministerial skills when they seem overqualified to shepherd small congregations anyway. But a sad fact of life is, "What you don't use, you lose." Although I took four years of French in high school and scored 96 percent on the statewide exam, now, twenty-some years later, the French on those famous Warner Brothers cartoons (*"Le skunk! Le pew! C'est une polecat! Runnez-vous!"*) sounds pretty good to me.

If you are not trying to grow as a pastor, you won't be able to retain even the level of competence you have now. And it will soon start to show. You'll answer a member of your congregation, "You want to study Ecclesiastes? Er, is that in the Bible?" When confronted with counseling situations, you'll be completely floored and find yourself asking, "What would Frasier Crane [TV sitcom psychologist] do if he were here?" You'll be helping a parishioner through a crisis of faith when you will suddenly realize that you are about to have one of your own. You'll lose the ability to tell whether or not a commentary is snowing you. As a matter of fact, you'll lose the ability to tell whether or not old Mrs. Johnson in the front row is snowing you.

We small-churchaholics desperately want a sense of closure in our lives. We want our counseling appointments with certain individuals to end. We wish we could say, "There! Now I've made the church healthy again. My job is done." We want to deal with board member Hi Percritical once and for all. But there is one area of our lives in which closure should never come: education. When seminary or Bible college end, your lifelong quest for knowledge is just getting started. If sharks stop swimming, they die. If rodents stop chewing, they die. If pastors stop learning. . . .

But you no longer have professors or ordination boards standing over you, giving you assignments, and setting deadlines. You've got to be your own professor and ordination board. As such, you'll want to make sure that you're receiving a well-rounded continuing education. To do this, you'll have to keep reading in all the disciplines that were part of your formal training: theology, church history, missions and evangelism, hermeneutics, church administration, pastoral counseling, Christian education, etc.

Now, before you get ready to crucify me, let me explain. I don't mean that you have to read books in all these fields all at once. Just pull a book off your shelf on, say, apologetics. Since you are your own professor, you can be flexible about the due date. After all, rank has its privileges. You can read the book a little bit at a time as you are able. If it takes you a week, fine. If it takes you a month, that's cool. Even if it takes you six months, who cares? The important thing is that you are slowly, surely, and steadily working to continue your education. After you finish that book, choose another from a different field and start in on that. Keep a record somewhere of the books you have read and review it from time to time to see if you are neglecting any important areas. We all have our favorite subjects. That's fine, but we won't be much good as pastors if we know everything about church-growth theory but not too much about eschatology (or vice versa). Small-church pastors are spiritual "general practitioners." We are expected to know a little bit about everything.

Beyond maintaining an accurate record, the reporting on your reading can be as simple or as complex as you'd like. Remember, you are your own professor. Make it easy on yourself! If you love to take notes on your reading, go to it! If you'd prefer to write a few sentences summarizing the main points of the book when you're finished, so be it! If you want to write full scale reviews or summary critiques, more power to you! Even if you don't want to write down anything, that's fine, too! Constant exposure to stimulating material will still have a positive effect on you. Just as you can't remember what was said in every single class during seminary, but the overall experience shaped you into who you are today, so it's not important to remember everything you read. Sometimes when I'm faced with a question or a problem, I will suddenly recall the day we talked about it in a class, or where in my notes and textbooks I can find the answer. The same thing happens with regards to my reading. I often will suddenly remember something I've read which speaks to a given situation, or I'll go scurrying over to my bookshelves because I know that author X had something helpful to say on the matter.

If a particular book is boring you or you lose interest in a subject, abandon it and consign the book back to the shelf. You don't have to feel obligated to finish it. At least you've done a little reading in that particular discipline. That's all that counts. If you are the type who starts and reads several books at once, either read several in the same discipline at once or feel free to vary the topics. Once again remember that you are designing an independent study course for yourself. It should be challenging, but not a burden to you. You know what it's like to be you. Be good to yourself.

Perhaps the idea of being your own spiritual leader disturbs you. When you fall into a pit of indifference, lethargy, doubt, or despair, you still look for someone else to pull you up out of it.

But you must face a cold, hard fact. As a small-churchaholic, no one will ever be able to give you help that really lasts, unless you first want to help yourself. Others may be able to throw you the occasional lifeline, but you've got to stop diving into the deep end. Others can give you bandages. You've got to stop cutting yourself. Are you really tired of living the way you're living or not? If so, then help yourself. Pastor yourself back to health.

EIGHT

Fragile—Handle With Care

After months of confrontation with, and threats from, his antagonists in the church, it looked to Pastor Jay Eli as though the
fight was finally over and he had won. The local judicatory of
his denomination, confused by the conflicting reports it had been
hearing about what was going on in Jay's church, called a special
meeting on a Saturday where it would hear both sides of the story
and then offer what counsel it could. The day long meeting
couldn't have gone better.

It became obvious to everyone attending that those who wanted
to bring charges against Jay didn't have a leg to stand on. Not only
that, but so many others in the church stood and testified that God
was really with Pastor Jay and that his ministry had made a positive
impact on their lives. The judicatory finally told the antagonists to
repent and to start to work with Jay instead of against him. It told his
supporters to keep standing with Jay and that it was sure that now
that this was all behind the congregation, God was going to do great
things in the church. Jay left the meeting walking on air. The next
day he flew even higher when he and his supporters had a prayer
meeting after the worship service that ended up lasting the entire
afternoon! The Spirit of God was present in a very real and powerful way. Now, there could be no doubt at all whose side God was
really on and it looked like there were nothing but glory days ahead.

However, when he got home Sunday evening, he received a
phone call from one of his friends. It seems that she had heard the

wife of Jay's chief antagonist saying after church that she was totally unsatisfied with the way the meeting had gone on Saturday. She would never work with Jay and would continue to do all in her power to make him leave the church. As Jay hung up the phone, an overwhelming feeling of fear swept over him. He tried to tell himself that it was silly to be afraid. There wasn't anything more this woman could really do. She would be placed under discipline if she persisted in her ways. Besides, God was with him! Or was he? Maybe Jay had just been fooling himself. If God was really at work, why didn't the problem go away? Suddenly, Jay knew that he just had to get out of there. He got into his car and drove and drove. As the miles wore on, his thoughts got darker and darker. What if everything bad that had happened in the church *was* really *his fault,* after all! By the time he pulled into a motel in the wee hours of the morning and checked into a room intending to spend some time in prayer, all that came from his heart and lips was, "Just go ahead and kill me, Lord. I've failed you more ways than I can count. I'm a miserable sinner and not fit to live, much less to be a pastor!"

Imagine for a moment that you were Jay's counselor. What would you tell him if he called you up from that motel room? Probably the same thing God essentially told Elijah (whose story I've been trying to echo) in 1 Kings 19, "Eat something, get some sleep, calm down and then we'll talk." God remembers what many small-churchaholics often forget. What seems to be depression, or spiritual warfare, or a moment of crisis, is sometimes just common symptoms of a person who has been on the go too long without rest or refreshment. All the prayer, Bible study, soul searching, and praise-worship singing in the world won't do you any good when what you really need is a nap or a good meal. The twin feelings that Elijah expresses in 1 Kings 19 are dead giveaways that you are reaching the end of your reserves—either "I'm slime" or "I'm great, everybody else is slime." If I'm mumbling, muttering, and rumbling around the house about what a terrible pastor I am or about the cruel trick of fate that placed a nice guy like me in a worthless, faithless, God-forsaken congregation like this, my wife will often say, "You need to lie down awhile," or "I think you're getting hungry. I better start supper." And she's right. A few hours later I will be wondering what I was so upset about.

And remember that God didn't come to Elijah in the powerful wind that tore mountains apart and shattered the rocks, nor in the earthquake, nor in the fire. Instead, the Lord was in the gentle whisper. If your emotions are roiling and boiling over God will not normally speak with you, even though at the time you may be asking, "What is God trying to say to me in all of this?" Instead, God will wait until you have calmed down before he deals with you. And one of the best ways to calm your emotions down is to calm your body down.

Gnostics in Practice

Small-churchaholics often function as practical gnostics. They act as if they believe that, as long as their souls are all right with God, they can abuse their bodies all they want and it won't affect them. So they stay out five to seven nights a week doing "the work of the Lord." They gulp down all their meals on the run. They never take a day off because the ministry is just "too important." The most exercise they ever get is putting their reference books back on the shelves or standing behind the pulpit for an hour on Sunday mornings. And then they wonder why they suffer from breakdowns and burnouts.

The Bible teaches that what our bodies do has a direct bearing on our spiritual health. That's why people in the Bible sometimes prostrate themselves before the Lord in prayer. It's hard to have a humble attitude when you're standing ram rod straight, chin up. When people repent in the Bible, they fast, beat themselves, put on sackcloth, and cover themselves with ashes. It's hard to truly repent if you're eating a hot fudge sundae in the air-conditioned comfort of your favorite restaurant while you are wearing the new designer outfit you just bought. And of course, Scripture teaches us that unless our inner faith works itself out in godly actions of the body, it is useless.

The link between my body and my spirit really hits home to me whenever I'm coming down with a sinus infection. A day or two before any actual symptoms appear, I feel as though a huge dark cloud has descended on my heart. I hate myself. I hate my church. I think blasphemous thoughts. I doubt God. And absolutely nothing I do can snap me out of it. My prayers seem to vanish into a black hole somewhere. I frantically try to figure out what's wrong with me. I start to wonder if I'm finally losing my mind. Then I'll wake up one morning with my head totally clogged, that familiar pressure behind and under my eyes, and that peculiar taste in my mouth. "Okay," I'll say, "That explains it. Nothing serious to worry about. Just another annoying sinus infection." The body was sick and so the spirit simply followed suit.

If we're going to keep our spirits healthy, then we must take care of our bodies. I'm not a doctor, nor do I play one on television, but I am going to briefly examine four areas where care is needed, but often neglected—*rest, nutrition, exercise, and sex.* Now, I know you're probably anxious to jump ahead to that last one, but I'm still going to start with rest.

It's a wonder to me why so many small-churchaholics, myself included, have such difficulty with the concept of rest when it's so clearly taught and emphasized in Scripture. As early as the second chapter of the Bible, God rested and made the seventh day holy because of it. Later, of course, he commanded the Israelites to keep the Sabbath as a day on which no work would be done. He even commanded that every seven years the land itself be given a rest. Jesus promised his weary followers that he would give them rest. And while the purpose of the Gospel writers is not to chronicle every time Jesus sacked out, we do find him asleep in the boat and resting at the well in Samaria because the journey had tired him. Why then do we always insist on pressing on even when the journey is too much for us?

We first need to recapture the idea of the Sabbath—spending one day a week totally away from our jobs. If you maintain that you simply can't do this, then you're setting yourself up as being wiser than God who commanded it. If that's the case, then you've got a more serious problem than being overworked.

Hopefully, though, you do want to obey the Lord and observe a Sabbath. How do you do it? You must do more than just walk away from your desk and close the office door. You need to advertise the fact to your congregation that you will be unavailable to them on your day off except in the case of an emergency. You need to turn the ringer off of your phone. Turn on your answering machine to take any emergency messages, but don't check it until evening. Then only return any calls that absolutely can't wait until the next day. It's important that you don't engage in your usual job-related activities, because, as John A. Sanford writes,

> The purpose of such a day is to enter into a new state of consciousness. By removing yourself from your usual surroundings and tasks you allow a new consciousness to take shape. But it is like swimming—you need to get all the way into the water. If the day is broken up by some official task, the new kind of consciousness that is beginning to develop is broken. That is why just a few hours off here and there do not renew us sufficiently. It takes longer than that for the invisible threads that connect us to our work to be relaxed so that new thoughts, new moods, new experiences, can find their way in.[1]

The new consciousness cannot take shape if you're going to spend your day off thinking of or talking about the church. That's work! In order to help us truly take a day away from the church, my wife and I have given each other permission to bring the other up short if Cobblestone is brought up. If she notices that far away look on my face, she can ask me, "Are you thinking about the church? Well, quit it. It's your day off." If she starts talking about a problem in the church, I can say to her, "That's church business. We'll deal with it later." When the family goes on vacation, the children have permission to charge me a quarter every time I mention the church. I can talk about the Lord, yes, but Cobblestone, no. This may all seem so forced and artificial, but it gets us in the habit of ignoring the church when we're off. Many Mondays (my day off) and vacation days have passed where Cobblestone is the farthest thing from our minds. (The only real catch is that we did have to explain to James and Abigail that if they baited Daddy they couldn't claim the quarter!)

When you do go back to work, be careful, as much as it depends on you, not to overschedule yourself. You know what sorts of meetings tire you out and which people in the church wear you out. Give yourself some "downtime" after them. Unless you don't have a family and are a real night owl, beware of scheduling too many evenings out a week. If you find yourself dozing off in the middle of your own sermon, or if you start to experience either of the emotional extremes that Elijah did, chances are you've been burning the candle at both ends and are quickly running out of wax. Cut back on the "after supper" appointments. Try visiting with people Saturday or Sunday afternoons instead. (I'll have more to say about the small-churchaholic's schedule next chapter.)

When it comes to nutrition, the four basic food groups for many small-churchaholics are *hamburgers, tacos, pizza, and chocolate* (for variety, chips or fries may be substituted for the tacos). There are several reasons for this. First, small-church pastors, like many other types of pastors, often have to eat on the go and fast food is nothing if not fast. Second, small-church pastors often meet with people during the lunch hour and, on a small-church pastor's salary, this is the best you can do. Third, ministry is very draining, sometimes offering little in the way of immediate rewards. The small-churchaholic chooses to reward him or herself with some tasty treats that are easy to obtain and require no preparation.

Unfortunately, as anyone who has ever taken a high school health class knows, this kind of diet isn't very good for you. A young man I knew moved away from home across the county to take a new job. He was a bachelor who wasn't real acquainted with the kitchen. Since he was busy trying to move into his new place while getting a feel for work, he ate out every meal. Without realizing it, he began ingesting a fried foods diet. About a week and a half later he woke up one morning extremely ill. He was so weak and dizzy that he couldn't even walk around his apartment. His thoughts were all fuzzy and muddled. He drifted in and out of a sleepy stupor all day. That night a friend came over, discovered the problem, and asked him what he had been eating lately. The friend was utterly shocked when the young man related his usual daily menu. The friend went out and bought some vegetables and fresh fruit. The young man dined on veggies and fruit salad and almost instantly began to feel better. He had been missing essential vitamins and minerals. Once they were replenished, he was able to function again.

It's amazing how fatigue, spiritual depression, and weird thinking can often be cured by simply taking a multiple vitamin pill each morning. Even better, try to get the nutrients you need naturally through a balanced diet. As anyone who has seen me in person will realize, I'm the last person on earth to tell you that you have to give up fast foods and tasty junky treats. Go ahead and enjoy them. But at other times, when you are not in a hurry or when you're fixing meals at home, make sure you include generous portions of healthy foods. Even when you have to dine out, why not choose healthier alternatives every once in a while? How about ordering a sub loaded with tomatoes, green peppers, onions, pickles, and lettuce? Why not try an all-veggie pizza? Take it from a meat-lover, they are not as bad as they sound. Many fast food restaurants are now adding salad bars. Why not get some fresh vegetables to go with that burger, or even (heresy of heresies) order just a salad every now and again *in place of* the burger? If you watch what you eat now, you won't have so much to work off later.

Speaking of that, you probably don't need me to lecture you about the health benefits regular exercise can bring—increased stamina, stronger heart, lower blood pressure, more restful sleep, longer life, etc.—others have said it all elsewhere. But there are two other benefits to small-churchaholics that I want to point out. *A good workout is often like a mini-vacation.* I may enter the health club with my mind awhirl with the concerns of the church, but once I start pumping iron, all I can think about is grinding out one more rep. It gives me a break for awhile. I often leave the gym feeling as though I don't have a care in the world. Working out also allows me to accomplish something concrete. In the small church, the results of my labors are often intangible or hard to measure. Not so with lifting weights. I can look at my chart and know that I've been able to lift more now than a week ago. I can see my muscles growing and becoming more defined. An improved golf score, a longer walk without feeling wiped out, or a victory in a racquet ball game can leave you with the feeling of a job well done.

As with a hobby (see chapter 5), choose an exercise that fits your likes and your budget. You may have to try out several types before you find the one(s) that you really enjoy. If you don't enjoy your exercise, you won't stick with it. And let's face it, as a small-church pastor, don't you have to do enough things that you don't want to do? Why add one more?

Finding time to exercise can be a challenge. Some pastors try to combine "work" with "pleasure." They will pray and meditate as they go for long walks. I've counseled people while hiking. A friend and I often walk briskly around the local mall as we share about our churches and discuss what it means to be a pastor.

As a small-church pastor, your personal daily schedule may be very flexible. Chances are you can make it to the health club during "off hours" when you don't have to wait for the machines and equipment. For example, if I go first thing in the morning, or from 11 A.M. to 1 P.M., or 4 P.M. to 6 P.M., I'll end up spending more time than I can really afford. But if I arrive at about two o'clock in the afternoon, the place is practically deserted.

You can also make use of a few minutes of "downtime" in the office. I have a pair of hand grips on my desk that I squeeze from time to time. Why not pace the room for a few minutes or do a couple of stretching exercises? You can even do some of your sermon research while standing up. Every little bit will help.

Time for the Two of Us

Now we come to the part of the discussion you've been waiting for. I'll start by quoting Scripture:

> The husband should fulfill his marital duty to his wife, and likewise the wife to her husband. The wife's body does not

belong to her alone but also to her husband. In the same way, the husband's body does not belong to him alone but also to his wife. Do not deprive each other except by mutual consent and for a time, so that you may devote yourselves to prayer. Then come together again so that Satan will not tempt you because of your lack of self-control (1 Corinthians 7:3–5).

These verses make it pretty clear that it is normally God's intention for husbands and wives to have sex regularly and to meet each other's sexual needs. And they make it clear that if this doesn't happen, there will be consequences.

The small-churchaholic who is "too busy" to spend time with his or her spouse is asking for trouble. As a small-church pastor, I become close with many women in our "church family." I receive plenty of hugs on Sunday mornings and, on the holidays, my share of kisses on the cheek. During counseling and even just chats in the hall where women open up the details of their lives and problems to me, I am with them when they are the most emotionally and psychologically vulnerable. And at these moments, I am, too, because I know these women (they aren't merely clients or parishioners) and I can feel their pain. My heart goes out to them. I just have to make sure that my body doesn't follow it and that my heart returns. If my relationship with my wife was unfulfilling or worse, practically nonexistent, I would be a prime candidate for an affair.

Not only that, but also I would find it very hard to concentrate on my work. When my family's schedule has been full and the church has been so busy that I haven't had time with my wife in a while, I become very antsy and cranky and irritable. I find that instead of thinking about the Lord, I spend my time thinking about sex. Times of meditation turn into times of indulging sexual fantasies. There's not much I can do to derail my one-track mind.

If I'm apart from my wife for very long, I'm depriving both her and me of one of the most pleasurable and effective means that God has given to reduce stress and tension, increase self-esteem, conquer depression, and promote a feeling of well-being.[2] Why would I want to neglect that? And if I am neglecting that, it's no wonder why I'm feeling so down all the time.

As I've said before, as a small-church pastor, your personal schedule may be very flexible. (Actually, I believe it *should* be very flexible—see the next chapter.) Sex doesn't have to be reserved for bedtime or Saturday night. Any time can be the right time as long as you and your spouse can have some relaxed moments together. Even if you are having one of those hectic kinds of weeks, take time to show affection to your spouse. It will make a big difference even if there's not enough time for sex.

Let It All Out

What you are feeling during the day is important. Emotions can make or break you. Taking care of your body is an important way to get your emotions under control, but so is allowing yourself to express those emotions. Too many small-churchaholics keep everything bottled up inside. Maybe they are ashamed of what they are feeling. Maybe they are laboring under the impression that the pastor must always be strong. Perhaps they are afraid that if they let a little emotion trickle out, the dam will burst and a torrent will follow. Maybe they've been so indoctrinated with that old evangelical illustration, "Faith is the engine, feelings are the caboose," that they think they can detach the last car and be done with feelings altogether. For whatever reasons, their hearts wind up like pressure cookers.

And, unfortunately, we're not as sturdily made as pressure cookers. Paul says that we have our treasures in jars of clay. Even a pressure cooker can explode. A jar of clay can be blown to smithereens. And all the king's horses and all the king's men won't be able to put the pieces back together again. To prevent that from happening, you've got to vent some of that pressure that's building up inside.

Don't be afraid to vent to God. In the Bible, he lets Abraham laugh at him (Genesis 17:17), Abraham and Moses bargain with him (Genesis 18:16–33; Exodus 4:10–16), Jacob wrestle with him and win (Genesis 32:22–32), Job complain to him (Job 7:11–21) and accuse him of being unjust (Job 9:14–35), the psalmist laments to him and expresses incredibly strong hatred toward his enemies (Psalm 109), Jeremiah express doubt, confusion, and frustration with him (Jeremiah 1:4–6; 12:1–4; 20:7–18), and Habakkuk question his love, righteousness, justice, and plans (Habakkuk 1:2–4, 12–2:1). Do you think he won't be able to handle your anxieties over the small-church ministry? Will he strike you dead because you admit that you have a hard time loving your antagonists? Will he turn away from you if you demand that he tell you exactly why he's placed you in a small out-of-the-way place like this? Read the Scriptures I listed above. Some of them sound downright blasphemous! Yet God was able to handle those strong words and emotions. He's big enough to handle anything you throw at him, too.

Don't forget to express positive emotions to the Lord as well. Often we are like the nine lepers that Jesus healed (Luke 17:11–19). After he has answered our prayers, we're so busy going on and doing the next thing that we forget to stop and say, "Thank you!" The Bible tells us to praise the Lord rather loudly (Psalm 47:1; 150). Paul urges us to "speak to one another with psalms, hymns and spiritual songs. Sing and make music in your heart to the Lord, always giving thanks to God the Father for everything, in the name of our Lord Jesus Christ" (Ephesians 5:19–20). It sounds to me as if we're expected to be giddy at times, not only in private, but also in public! Why not go ahead and let yourself get caught up in the worship service and your own sermon? Rejoicing in the Lord will do your heart good, and having an enthusiastic pastor may be just what your staid, dry congregation needs to come back to life again.

You don't need to be afraid of letting your emotions out in front of others. Though some advocate maintaining a professional detachment from your people, this doesn't work in a small church. The people in a small church like to view themselves as one big family, as friends who know and care about each other. If a stranger makes an appointment for counseling and begins to tell me about her marital problems, I could probably grab my legal pad, pick up my pen, and say, "Just the facts, Ma'am." If it's my sister who's telling me her troubles, my heart is going to break. I'm going to cry along with her. If I'm visiting a man in the hospital who's just a name to me on the church roll, I'll be polite, attentive, express the proper amount of sympathy, read a few Scriptures, pray, and leave. If it's my friend lying there, I'm probably going to blurt out, "Man! What happened to you? Are you okay?"

If I receive a report that several new babies were born in the congregation, I might say, "That's nice," and instruct my secretary to send out the proper congratulatory form letters. If I hear that Rod and Sarah just had their baby, I'll let out a whoop and rush right down to the hospital to see the little fellow. The small church expects me to enter into its joys and sorrows. God expects it, too. Romans 12:15 says, "Rejoice with those who rejoice; mourn with those who mourn." The small-church pastorate puts me in a position where I can do just that.

I can even share my negative emotions with others. Obviously, I don't share all of them. I am an adult, after all, and adults don't cry and carry on every time they are disappointed or things don't go their way. I also know that I have to be "as wise as a serpent and as harmless as a dove." Neither do I share with just anybody. Some aren't mature enough in their own faith to be able to handle the fact that the pastor gets discouraged. Some aren't called to bear the burdens of interchurch politics. And some just can't be trusted. But I am supposed to be friends with those in my congregation and friends let friends know what's on their minds. Many a small church has been shocked when a pastor resigns and even more so when they hear his or her reasons. Nobody knew anything was wrong. There's a sense of betrayal. "I thought he or she was our friend! If so much was really bothering the pastor, why didn't he or she just say so. Maybe we could have worked out our differences together." And maybe not. At least they like to think that they would have tried. Why not give them the opportunity? Then if things still don't work out, you can part as friends going your separate ways, rather than as people who have stabbed each other in the backs. Withholding negative emotions leads to ulcers, heart attacks, and migraines. Letting them out gives them and their root causes the opportunity to be dealt with. It lets healing occur. (See chapter 6 for more on sharing with others.)

A pastor is not Superman, vulnerable only to magic and kryptonite. Unfortunately, you can be put out of commission by the common cold. Satan doesn't need to build an exotic doomsday device powered by red sun radiation to take away your powers. All he needs to do is to get you so busy "doing the work of the Lord" that you neglect to take care of yourself.

You have your treasure in a jar of clay. Take care of it and it will take care of you.

NINE

Two-Timing the Day-Timer

uestion: How is being a small-church pastor like being an emergency room nurse or a parent?

Answer: When you're on the job, you never know what will happen next.

An emergency room nurse doesn't know what kind of shift he or she is going to have. Who can tell how many people are going to walk in or be carried through that door and when? What kind of conditions will they be in? It's impossible to tell in advance, so every day or night on the job is like a brand-new adventure.

Being a parent is full of unexpected surprises as well. For example, last night my wife and I planned to relax in front of the television, but shortly after our six-year-old daughter went to bed, she began to throw up. Our plans were forgotten as we spent the rest of the evening taking care of her. It sure wasn't the kind of night we expected, but when you are a parent, it's impossible to predict what's going to happen next and plan accordingly. You have to be flexible and take things as they come.

It's the same if you are a small-church pastor. You are called to be nurse, doctor, parent, friend, confidant, counselor, and trouble-shooter to a group of people. It's impossible for you to predict what your week is going to be like. You're just going to have to go with the flow.

When I started out in the ministry, I tried to stick to a weekly schedule. After all, I had heard that successful people take control of their lives and manage their time well. I certainly wanted to be successful, so I sat down and blocked out time each week for devotions, long-range planning, sermon preparation, administration work, visitation, meetings, and appointments. I thought I knew how much time I would need in each area in order to do my job well and I made sure I gave myself that time.

However, real life intruded into my carefully made plans and messed them up royally. A severely troubled young person had joined our congregation. The elders and I tried to help this individual straighten out her life (cue the theme from *Mission: Impossible*). We soon got drawn into encounters with the police, angry neighbors, creditors, neo-Nazis, social workers, and parishioners who had been cheated or hurt by her. Once one of my elders and I drove all over the city playing "detective," trying to find where she'd been hiding from the social workers, the cops, and us for a couple of days. At one point, the elder looked over at me and gave a weary laugh, "I'll bet when you were in seminary you never once imagined that you'd be spending your time in the ministry like this." No, I hadn't, and I certainly never made room for this sort of thing on my schedule. In fact, one of my frustrations with the whole affair was that I could spend most of the week "on the job" and yet, according to my schedule, have gotten "nothing" done!

On top of all that, I also quickly discovered that my people weren't impressed with having a "busy pastor" and became disappointed or upset if I was a little short with them on the phone or in person because I had other things to do. As Nancy T. Foltz writes,

> In general small churches are usually informal—and want the pastor to be also. Suggestions like, "Why don't you call the office and make an appointment to see me?" may be offensive to some. Pastors who are loved by small congregations are usually those willing to be available in the grocery store and the post office as well as the church office. The highly relational nature of the small church encourages accessibility.[1]

So, once again, I often found that while I was spending a large part of my day with my people, according to my schedule, I was falling behind in my work.

As a small-churchaholic, I, of course, felt guilty that somehow, according to my master plan, I wasn't doing my job. Yet I also was very confused because I knew I was spending my time in ministry. I certainly wasn't watching game shows, soap operas, and *Gilligan's Island* reruns all day! I didn't want to live with these levels of guilt, confusion, and frustration. What was I going to do?

For one thing, I needed a new way to plan my week and evaluate my time. I stopped blocking out time for each task. Now, I simply make a list of all the tasks I *have* to do along with those I would *like* to do on one sheet of paper each week. I keep in mind the difference between what absolutely has to get done and what would be nice if it were done. For example, I absolutely have to prepare and preach a sermon every week. It would be nice if I had some time to dream dreams about the church's future, but it's not essential that I do so *this week.* I include absolutely everything I can on the list, even the seemingly insignificant (sort through church mail, take the bulletin to the copy shop, change the letters on the church sign, etc.). Then, whenever I complete a task, I put a check mark through it.

In some cases, I put a check mark through some things if I've found even just a moment to work on it. I may not have been able to spend two hours writing up a new Christian education policy, but I did spend fifteen minutes. If I can do that for a few weeks running, I'll have that policy. It may be that I couldn't spend a lot of time in long-range planning, but at least I spent some. It should then be checked off the list so I won't look over the week and moan, "I didn't get a chance to prepare for the future!"

When interruptions occur, I immediately write them on the list and check them off.

"Phone call from Mr. Smith about changing the day of our garbage pick-up."—Wrote down. Checked off.

"Mrs. Jones shows up with a copy of a new song she heard on the radio and wants to know if our choir can work it up. She stays awhile and chats about her elderly mother whom she recently had to put in a nursing home."—Right. Checked off.

"Found out about Larry Jackson being admitted to the hospital. Hopped in the car and drove right over."—After writing it down and checking it off, of course.

Thus, when I come to the end of a day or week and wonder, "What did I really do?" I can consult my list and remember. If I want to know why I wasn't able to get to all the tasks I initially wrote down on the list, I can consult the amended list and understand. "Oh, yeah. I had to do some grief counseling with the Baker's, track down our missing vacation Bible school supplies, and drive Widow Miller to a doctor's appointment."

Whenever I find myself having some "free" moments during the day, whether several minutes or several hours, I can consult my list and choose a task or tasks to start or complete. I can put in twenty minutes on my sermon today, forty tomorrow, without wasting time lamenting that on Wednesday, from 1 to 4 P.M., I didn't get my scheduled three hours with the commentaries.

At the end of a week, if I've accomplished the absolutely essential, I can feel successful. Any tasks on the list that remain untouched or unfinished get automatically transferred to the following week's list. If many weeks go by and I notice the same chores remain untouched and yet nobody is ever inquiring about them, I can safely assume that they really aren't all that important to me or my current ministry and drop them off the list (and out of my mind) for good. (Or at the very least, for a little while.)

Some things may be important, just not right now. If I can't find it within myself to drop a task entirely, I turn the pages on my calendar ahead three months and write it down on the top of the page. In three months time, I can revisit the whole thing and perhaps begin putting it on my weekly lists again.

There may be certain times during the year when action in your church slows up a bit. (Hint: I'm not talking about from Thanksgiving to Christmas or during Lent.) These periods are ideal for doing research, planning, and writing. From about the second Sunday in June through the first Sunday in September is such a time at Cobblestone. It's remarkable that when the weather turns (however briefly) mild in the Northeast, suddenly nobody needs to talk to the pastor anymore! I can usually get some things done in the summer that I've had to put off the rest of the year. It's getting now so that I save myself some grief and just go ahead and schedule them for the summer to begin with.

No Nine-to-Five Job

I can also save myself a lot of needless grief by keeping in mind that the pastorate is not a forty-hour-a-week, nine-to-five job. Some weeks will require that I put in over forty. The small-church-aholic in me immediately wants to feel cheated: "I didn't get enough time off. I'm not getting paid overtime." Other weeks are kind of slow, and I can find myself putting in fewer hours. The small-churchaholic in me immediately begins feeling as though I'm cheating the congregation. "I'm not giving the church its money's worth. I'm not a faithful servant. I'm lazy!" I may even begin trying to think up things to do. *Warning:* there is nothing more dangerous than a small-church pastor who is trying to come up with something to do. You'll start to think up futile schemes to change your congregation into something it doesn't want to be, or dream up a grandiose future for your church that will ultimately frustrate you when it fails to come to pass, or muster up the courage to finally put that antagonist in his place only to have his friends put you in yours, or overmanage your poor, overworked volunteers.

It's better to realize and accept that, as a pastor, you don't have to punch a time clock and never will. You are a professional, and many professionals keep very different schedules from blue-collar workers. My father was a high school mathematics teacher. While he had to be at the school certain hours every day, I know he also put in long hours at home at night doing lesson plans and grading papers. During final exams week, Dad often worked several days straight without much of a break. Not to mention the work he did over the years coaching and supervising sporting events. Any teacher who believes "I put in my eight hours and now I'm outta here," is fooling him or herself. I know that some-times teachers are criticized (or perhaps envied) because they get to take summers off. Well, having observed Dad, I would say that the extra hours he worked during the rest of the year more than evened things out.

The farmers in the area where I grew up also didn't have strict nine-to-five jobs. They went all out from spring through fall, putting in twelve hour or longer days during harvesting seasons. But during the winter, they had much more time to relax. Many took off and spent the months vacationing in Florida. My point is that many jobs have periods of intense activity followed by calmer times of rest. The pastorate is no different. Don't feel guilty about following its ebb and flow.

You're going to have heavier weeks—several committee meet-ings, a funeral for a long-time member, Edna's getting a heart transplant, the newsletter deadline is here, etc. Resign yourself to the fact that sleep, or even just time to put your feet up, may be hard to come by. Just push yourself through. (Why do you think the Lord places caffeinated beverages at church gatherings any-way?) Also, as soon as it becomes evident that you're going to have a hectic week, take all of the nonessential items on your list and put them on the following week's. Concentrate only on the essentials. Even then, you may want to change Sunday's sermon text to one you know cold and can preach on without a lot of advance preparation. The congregation will probably understand last minute changes in a week where there was a "family crisis" for the church. They'll appreciate the time you spent visiting in the hospital or attending the wake more than the time you'd spend studying behind your desk.

You're going to have lighter weeks—almost everybody is out of town on vacation, nobody's in the hospital, the next holiday is two months away, the board meeting was canceled for lack of a quorum, etc. Use the time to recover from the heavier weeks. Don't be afraid to write down "Recovery Time" on your list and then check it off. Write next to it all the things you are recovering from if you really must. (Some of you small-churchaholics are incorrigible.) Take naps. Go for a walk. Rent a movie. And don't feel guilty about it! Remember your need for rest (see the previous chapter). If you have a hard time shaking the guilt over taking a salary when you're not doing much of anything, remember that you are still on call. Just because the phone isn't ringing at the moment doesn't mean it won't start in the next sixty seconds. You are being paid to be available to "the family" when it needs you. And "the family" will expect you to be refreshed and energized enough to be able to help out when the call comes. Get yourself ready for that next emergency by relaxing now.

You can also relieve some of the false guilt during a light week by catching up on some of those items that have remained untouched week after week on your list. Just don't overwork yourself. You'll do no one any good in the long run if you make every week into a heavy week.

I often find that even during an average week (not too heavy, not too light, just right!) I need to take mini-vacations away from it all. If I've just finished counseling a woman in our close-knit church family who's found out she has breast cancer, I may be too shaken up to immediately pick up my pen and begin writing my sermon. I may need to leave my desk for awhile, regardless of whether or not I've yet put in my eight hours that day. A short drive, a visit with a friend, or a quick board game with my children may be just what I need to calm down and get my feelings under control so that I may minister again.

I don't have to feel guilty about "abandoning my post." I'm actually taking care of myself so that I can remain "at my post." My Lord and Savior Jesus Christ did the same thing. He withdrew from the crowds in order to find strength from God to continue in his mission. In Mark 1:35–37, he goes off by himself to pray, even though everybody in town is looking for him to make demands on his time. Jesus didn't carry a cellular phone or have "call-forwarding" or a pager. It wasn't just that these things hadn't been invented yet. I don't believe that Jesus would have these things if he was bodily on earth today. He was only at the beck and call of God, not of people.

Many small churches try to keep their pastors at their beck and call by insisting that the pastor keep regular office hours. This leads to situations like the pastor, having crawled out of bed after a meeting that dragged on until midnight and an adrenaline high that didn't let him crash until 3 A.M., driving to the church, going into his office, closing the door, and sacking out on the floor. He would have preferred to be sleeping in his nice, soft bed, but at least now his car can be seen in the parking lot and everyone will know the pastor is in. Or how about the "sports fan" pastor who smuggles her television set into the office so she won't miss that important Saturday afternoon game. Or the pastor who leaves the office light on and the soft music playing while he sneaks down to the local convenience store for a candy bar.[2]

Why not just be honest and up front about the fact that you really don't want to have office hours? It doesn't have to be stated in a negative way. Here is how I put it to search committees: "I've never found office hours to work very well in a small church. Even though I might be at the office from 8 A.M. until 4 P.M., I'm willing to bet I would still get phone calls at home at night, when supposedly I was off duty, about church business and people's problems. After all, evenings are when you folks are at home and have the time to call. I understand that and certainly don't want to resent you for it. Also, I don't want to ever cut short time I'm spending with any of you because I feel I have to get back to the office. And being with you in a crisis situation may entail me being away from my desk for hours on end.

"Office hours don't really fit the way I work or the way I'm built. I sometimes get ideas for sermons or Bible studies when I wake up in the middle of the night. I might jot down a few thoughts or even get up and work a while.[3] Would you expect me the next day to put in hours 'doing my work?' My work may already be done! I bounce ideas around while I'm preparing meals, taking a shower, or whatever. I can often be found writing or reading about the church during 'off' time at home. When I attend meetings at night it always takes me several hours afterward to wind down and get to bed—even if it was a good meeting. I'm not good for much early the next morning. I'd probably fall asleep at my desk.

"How about if instead of office hours, we just let everyone know that they can call me at any time? If I'm not there, they can leave a message and I'll call them back as soon as I can. I want to be accessible to everyone. If it ever gets to the point where the board feels I'm not accessible or that I'm not getting my work done, let me know and I'll try keeping office hours again."

Small churches usually respond well to this because it fits in with the spontaneous, informal, friendly way they do things. And I've stressed that I want to be accessible. Bottom line: That's all they really want, too.

Current technology has gone a long way toward making the small-church pastor's office hours obsolete anyway. Many small churches in the past asked their pastor to keep regular hours so that someone would be in the church to answer the phone and/or so that the congregation would have easy, ready access to the pastor at least part of the week. But with answering machines, E-mail, and voice mail, people can now convey their messages to me even when I'm not around. Churches using recorded announcements or web pages can impart all the necessary information about themselves that a potential visitor would need, even though he or she never once talks to a "live" human being. For a time, these advances were resisted particularly by the older generation who didn't want to "talk to some dumb machine," but now, as I'm phoning the elderly members of my congregation, I'm noticing that more and more of them have those "dumb machines."

Squarely on My Shoulders

Not having office hours puts the burden of having a ministry of integrity squarely where it belongs, on my shoulders. For all the congregation knows, I could be pulling old sermons out of the files and spending all my time fiddling with my comic book collection. I have to admit that at times the temptation is definitely there. But I would rather wrestle with it and be answerable to God than to be answerable to a group of people who have no idea what kind of week I'm having, but use as their criterion of what makes a good pastor whether I make it into the office every Monday, Wednesday, and Friday from 9 A.M. to noon and 1 to 2:30 P.M.

Something that helps keep me honest and gives the board a clearer picture of my ministry than punching an artificial time clock is my monthly visitation report. At every elders meeting, I let my leaders know how many pastoral visits I've made since the last meeting. The visits are sorted into categories. "Hospital Visits" are pretty self-explanatory, as are "Shut-in Communions." "Home Visits," though, refer not only to official visits in people's homes or visits they make to my office (which is in my home), but also to times I've met people at the mall, or the supermarket, or in the hall after church and chatted about their lives or their faith. I don't count times where we've only talked about the weather, or the new movie, or our kids, etc., but only those times when I have acted as a pastor, answering questions, offering counsel, promising support. "Phone Visits" are similar. I don't count a phone call asking me what time the Sunday school picnic is as a "visit," but if that same caller would also express concern over the direction of the church and dialog with me about it, or would tell me about marriage problems he or she was having, or would say, "As long as I've got you on the phone, I've been meaning to ask you who exactly the 'sons of God' in Genesis 6 are?" then it counts. The discipline of keeping track of my visits helps to constantly remind me what being a pastor is all about.

It's about serving my people in the name of Christ, helping them grow as his disciples, and reminding them of his presence, love, perseverance, and power. To the extent that day-timers, calendars, and personal planners can help me do this, they are valuable. When they become an obstacle to ministry, they need to be shown the circular file. If office hours help you minister Christ, by all means keep them. If they are an unnecessary burden, jettison them at once.

TEN

To Thine Own Self Be True

Here's something I bet you never expected an author to say: "If anything in this book doesn't fit your personality, experience, congregation, temperament, or style of ministry, PLEASE FEEL FREE TO IGNORE IT!" I mean it! I didn't write this book to try to pressure you into becoming like me. I don't want to be yet another voice telling you what, as a pastor, you have to be or do. I wrote the book in the hope of freeing you from those voices and giving some food for thought so that you can determine just exactly who you are in the ministry.

A wise older pastor took me aside when I was just starting out in the pastorate and told me he knew what the most important task was that I would have to accomplish in my first five years of ministry. If I was expecting to hear, "Develop a devotional life," or "Become a real people person," or "Run annual stewardship campaigns," or "Get your congregation excited about evangelism," I was to be disappointed. Instead, he told me, "The most important thing you'll do in the first five years is to discover who Steve Bierly is as a pastor."

When I expressed bewilderment as to what he was getting at, he laughed and asked me, "Aren't there books in your library that deep down inside you know you'll never read, but you were guilt-tripped into buying anyway? You heard, 'every thinking pastor needs a copy of thus-and-so,' and you ran right out to buy one." He shared with me that he used to have older books by some of the classic theologians in his study, but that he was now selling them because he finally had admitted to himself that they always put him to sleep. Why shouldn't he buy more contemporary books and commentaries that he would actually use, even if they wouldn't look as impressive on the shelves? He didn't subscribe to every Christian magazine or journal either, even though, pastors were supposed to always be "up" on everything. He only ordered what he would read.

He also shared with me that he no longer got all dressed up in a shirt, tie, and suit coat to make hospital calls. He had a very friendly, open, relaxed, "one of the guys" style of ministry, and putting on a "costume" just wasn't him. Instead, he went with a neat, clean, but casual look.

Not that my friend was being selfish. In fact, he is one of the most sacrificing pastors I've ever known. But he realized that the ministry was hard enough without adding the burden of constantly trying to be something or someone you aren't. Those who try to carry that extra weight wind up with ulcers, migraines, and bouts with depression.

Carrying the Burden

I know that lugging that burden around nearly destroyed me. The first congregation I pastored didn't know quite what to make of a young, single pastor. I definitely loved the Lord, but I also enjoyed movies, dating, video games, and rock 'n' roll. While some in the church participated in these activities with me, others definitely showed their discomfort that a "holy man" would engage in such things. I also heard comments about the way I dressed, my apartment, and whom I chose to have over. It wasn't long before I started to hide my private life from the people and adopt more of a "Pastor Steve" persona. Also, the congregation had a "by the book" way of doing things, and I was more of a hang-loose, live-and-let-live type of guy.

In order to work with my elders and minister in that church, I had to try to adapt to their style. But it was a pretty tight, uncomfortable fit. Doctrinal and denominational distinctives were extremely important to that congregation. As a result, sermons and

Bible studies which focused on these were what was expected of me. I found myself trying to find ways to cram the five points of Calvin, or the presbyterian form of government, or the evils of secular society into messages where they didn't really belong. Every time I got up to preach or teach I felt like I was locked inside a straitjacket. Not that the congregation was necessarily wrong in their corporate personality, their pastoral expectations, or the way they viewed their mission, but it certainly wasn't for me.

As a result, my irritable bowel got worse. I found myself sleeping a lot. I felt guilty over both doing my work and not doing my work, and I often felt disconnected from life. It was as though I was standing off at a distance, outside of my body, watching this creature named Steve go through the motions. My relatively new bride became concerned as she noticed the changes in me, but she knew that because I was a loyalist at heart, I didn't want to abandon the Lord's call or wimp out during trying times. It would be difficult for me to consider the possibility of moving on. So, she confided in three of my closest friends from seminary whom I loved and trusted, and they almost immediately drove up and paid me a visit. It helped shock me back to my senses when these dear people told me in tears that I was no longer the Steve Bierly they knew. I was becoming someone or something else entirely and they didn't like it. More importantly, they could see that the metamorphosis was killing me.

A short time later, we traveled on vacation to my family reunion. My wife left the gathering that afternoon in tears and I followed her to find out what was wrong. She said, "Steve, you're so relaxed here. You're not fighting to belong. You just *do* belong. Your sense of humor is coming back. In fact, I see you waking up from the ministerial stupor. I just wish it could be like this all the time." Right then and there I made a vow to her that either things would change in the ministry we were in or we would move as quickly as possible.

Immediately after we returned from vacation, things got immeasurably worse. Conflicts with the leadership over ministry style, outreach plans, and vision for the future that had been simmering came to a full boil. This time, rather than staying and try-ing to find compromises, I left for good. Although I missed some of the people, was grateful for the experiences I had there, and appreciated the way that even some of my antagonists had stood by and helped me during transitions in my life (marriage, the birth of my son), I never regretted saying good-bye. I had learned that one has to listen to family and friends and that one has to find a ministry where one can truly be oneself and be at home.

Not that friends and family are always right (see Mark 3:20–21, 31–34, for example). And you don't have to remain the class cutup that they remember from junior high. Hopefully you will mature along the way, but your friends and family should be able to tell if you are becoming a more adult, more stable, more sea-soned version of that adolescent, or if you are mutating into who-knows-what. They will be sensitive to whether you are being refined by the pressures of ministry or melting down to nothing.

It's not that you won't, from time to time, even in the best min-istries, have to assume roles that make you uncomfortable and do tasks that seem better suited for somebody else. It's the nature of the job and part of what it means to be willing to sacrifice for Jesus. But you don't have to be in a ministry that pressures you to take the Self, which God has created, trained, and shaped, and throw it away. Not even the leaders in the Bible did that. While it's true that the apostle Paul took into account his audiences' tastes, lifestyles, and backgrounds and changed his approach and even his way of life to minister to different groups, he always did so with a strong sense of his personal mission. He was adopting different personas as a means to save some. He didn't do it out of fear of confrontation, or a desire to please everyone, or the need to keep a job. He did it because it fit in with his understanding of who he was at his core—the Apostle to the Gentiles. He knew that his actions didn't clash with his bedrock identity.

Not all of the rest of the apostles ministered effectively to Gen-tiles. Why not? It seems as though some didn't have the gifts nec-essary to be cross-cultural missionaries. They probably would have been miserable trying to do what Paul did. Rather than painfully and vainly attempting to be square pegs in round holes "for Jesus," they concentrated mainly on ministry to the Jews. I, therefore, see nothing biblically wrong with trying to find a field of ministry that allows you to be yourself.

Up from the Ashes of Disappointment

How do you find one? Why not begin by being totally yourself and as honest as you can be with a search committee or a congregation that expresses interest in having you as their pastor? The candidating process is much like going on a first date with someone you desperately want to impress. He or she says, "I love to ski," and you find yourself saying, "Me, too," even though you've never worn a pair of skis in your life. Why not instead say, "Not me. I'm into other things." Be upfront with a church from the very start about what it can expect of you as a pastor, what you believe, how you like to spend your free time, how you're going to make sure you get some free time, the level of involvement your family will have in the church, etc. The pain of being turned down by a few congregations until you find the right one is nothing compared to the pain of having to leave a church because you find out down the road that the "marriage" was built on an illusion and you and your "mate" are really incompatible.

And why not reveal a little bit about yourself in your candidating sermons? You could use illustrations that are drawn from your hobbies. For example, I may say that I'm fanatical about old movies and then use a scene from a film to make a point. Why not include part of your testimony in the sermon and let the congregation find out about your background? Tell the congregation about a time your spouse or children helped you find strength in the Lord. This way they can get to know your family as well. Share a little bit of your dreams for the church. Quote from your favorite hymn or passage from a Christian author, offering a brief explanation as to why it's your favorite. Give your potential flock a chance to understand a little of what makes you tick. If they hire you, they'll be hiring the real you. If they reject you, you'll be better off than if you had come into a group that doesn't really want *you*.

It's possible to go overboard with self-references in any sermon. The purpose of the message is to point to Jesus, of course, and not yourself. However, it is biblical to share with your listeners not only the gospel, but your life as well (1 Thessalonians 2:8). The Lord does use personal testimony to bring down Satan (Revelation 12:11). There will almost always be people present in the worship service for whom your personal stories will hit home. Many have appreciated it when I have shared how, although I grew up as a good, middle-class, "church kid," I still came to the realization that I was a sinner and needed the Lord. They, too, weren't drug dealers, gangsters, or drunkards, but they were lost nonetheless until Jesus found them.

When I reveal myself, even my weaknesses, to the congregation, it often enhances my ministry. In one church I pastored, a young woman came to the Lord under my preaching and subsequently developed quite a case of "hero worship." Pastor Bierly knew everything and could do no wrong in her eyes. But I still remember the day the glow in those eyes faded. It was visibly noticeable and it happened within a matter of seconds. She had entered my office for the first time and saw all my bookshelves.

"What are all these books for?" she asked suspiciously.

"I use them to do the research to prepare for my sermons and Bible studies."

"You mean you don't just know all that stuff you say right off the top of your head?" She was crestfallen.

"Nope! Not at all. But look at the bright side. You, too, can know all that stuff. Let me show you a few books that can help you get started."

Out of the ashes of her disappointment rose an expectation that she could grow to be just like Pastor Steve! And isn't this the whole point of the ministry? We're not to show off to others how great we are or to snow them into thinking we're living on a higher spiritual plane than they could ever reach, but to tell others, "All I am I owe to Jesus. He showed me how to grow in faith, knowledge, and love. I can share what I've learned with you. You can grow, too!" As time went on my wife and I opened up to the young woman about some of our spiritual struggles, as she did with us about hers. We appreciated her prayerful support and listening ear. She was now a friend. She was now our Christian sister instead of a puppy dog rolling around at the feet of her "spiritual master."

Revealing myself to the people of Cobblestone has proved to be a pleasant surprise. I suspected during the candidating process that I would find acceptance here, but it constantly amazes me that the more I reveal about myself, the more they say, "That's okay. That's cool." I remember that I approached my first talent show here with a little trepidation. How would the good people respond when they saw their pastor dressed as Elvis or imitating Bob Dylan? Well, they rolled on the floor laughing. They loved it. I sometimes do some pretty outrageous things in my children's sermons (like doing a rap song or putting peanut butter on my face), but the messages are always well received. After I had used my comic book collection to present the gospel message at a youth group overnight, one of the mothers asked her daughter how Pastor Steve's collection was. "It's his life!" she replied, and the people standing around the church who heard her responded with affectionate laughter and good-natured glances in my direction.

Hallelujah, Either Way

My point in telling you all of this is not to say, "Nyah! Nyah! I found a good church. Too bad you didn't!" Rather, I want to encourage you to begin sharing your true self with your current congregation despite any fears. You have nothing to lose by taking off the cumbersome iron mask and revealing your true face. If the congregation accepts you, Hallelujah! You've found a home. If they reject you, Hallelujah! Now you can feel free to pray and look for another call without guilt! Now you don't have to keep expending large amounts of energy trying to be someone else.

Of course, it's not only congregations that pressure us to give up our identities. We put the pressure on ourselves. We hear about the great Christian leaders of the past and become depressed and discouraged because we can't be just like them. Once after read-

ing that many of them used to get up at the crack of dawn and
spend hours in prayer, I decided to set my alarm a little earlier and
begin my day with God. In reality, it turned out that I began each
day with sleepy hallucinations, jumbled thoughts, mumbled
prayers mixed with large doses of snoring, and a huge helping of
guilt. Then it was pointed out to me that the normal average bedtime for men like Luther, Calvin, and the Puritans was 8:30 P.M. or
9 P.M. at the latest. That's why they could rise and shine at 5 A.M.

When you closely examine the great heroes of the church you
will quickly discover that they were not superhumans "with powers and abilities far beyond those of mortal men" but, rather,
people much like yourself, with strengths, to be sure, but many
weaknesses, too. John Wesley wasn't much of a husband. Charles
Spurgeon was prone to depression. Jonathan Edwards was a difficult person to live with. G. K. Chesterton's strong, rational faith
grew out of a life of inner turmoil and personal suffering.

Just as I didn't want the young woman in my church to put me
up on a pedestal, but rather to see that she, with God's help, could
be like me, so we must realize that the "great" in "the great men
and woman of the faith" was God, the same God who lives in us
today. Even in the Bible, the only true, consistent hero is God.
Abraham was willing to give up his wife in order to save his own
skin. Jacob was a liar and a cheater. Moses was hot-headed. David
was an adulterer, a murderer, and one who, while ruling Israel,
certainly couldn't manage his own family. Jeremiah acted like a
manic-depressive. Mary tried to dissuade Jesus from the ministry.
Peter was a braggart and a coward. The same John who wrote,
"God is love," wanted to call fire down on unbelievers, and
wanted to be a big shot in the kingdom of God. The same Paul
who wrote that the most important thing is love, that we must strive
to live at peace with everybody, and that we should consider others as being better than ourselves, broke up with his friend and
advocate, Barnabas, when they had a major disagreement.

The stories in the Bible are told, not so that we will sit around
moping because we're not apostles, but rather so we can say, "If
God can use sinners like them, he can use me, too!" You don't

have to be someone else in order to accomplish great things, you just have to have the help of Someone else.

In seeking to be yourself, never forget that if you are really called by God to the ministry, then a large part of who you are is being a pastor. Your identity is not solely bound up in your hobbies and "outside life," with the ministry, then, being an imposition on the "real you."

There is a comic book that tells the story of Batman's early career. As Bruce Wayne is preparing to become the Caped Crusader, he tells his butler and confidant, Alfred, that he will need different costumes for the changing seasons.

"You'll be continuing this masquerade into the warmer months?" Alfred asks.

Bruce replies, "The Batman is *not* a masquerade, Alfred. It is my life's *mission*."[1]

The pastorate is *not* a masquerade for you. It is your life's mission. Therefore don't be surprised if, as you're watching a movie or television show, you find yourself evaluating what it's saying about the beliefs of our modern culture or planning how to use parts of it as sermon illustrations. Don't get too uptight if, while on vacation, you still find yourself drawn into conversations about faith and the state of the church today. You're not cracking up if, in the middle of a tennis match, you suddenly pray a quick prayer for a parishioner in the hospital. If you sit down to a good meal and the phone rings, view this as a *continuation* of your life, instead of as an interruption of it.

This is not to say you can never take a break from the ministry. Much of this book, of course, has been about how to do just that. But our attitude should be the same as Christ's in Mark 6:30–34. The disciples had just returned from their missionary journeys and were reporting to Jesus. However, "so many people were coming and going that they did not even have a chance to eat." So Jesus said to the twelve, "Come with me by yourselves to a quiet place and get some rest." (Notice that it's not wrong to get away from it all every once in a while. Jesus even advocates it.) They set out in a boat to travel to a solitary place, but when they arrived, there was the crowd again! What was Jesus' reaction? Did he grumble? Did he tear his hair out yelling, "Why can't you people go away and leave us alone?" Did he curse? No, the Scripture says, "He had compassion on them, because they were like sheep without a shepherd. So he began teaching them many things." Christ was overcome with love for the needy and so he was true to himself and continued his life's mission. When unexpected "interruptions" occur, try to let yourself be motivated by Christ's love for the needy people who are contacting you and get on with your life's mission.

A foodaholic can't give up eating. He or she needs food in order to stay alive. The foodaholic just needs to learn proper eating habits, how to manage food, and balancing his or her desires correctly. The small-churchaholic can't really ever give up the pastorate. He or she needs to minister in order to stay spiritually alive. The small-churchaholic just needs to learn how to properly handle the pastorate.

I have faced the fact that pastoring will always be a part of me. I once briefly took a so-called "part-time" church in order to catch my breath after a particularly draining ministry. Even though I was only supposed to work twenty hours a week and had been advised, "Keep track of your time and don't give them anything they aren't willing to pay for," I found myself spending a lot of my "time off" dreaming dreams and making plans for that congregation. When people called me for appointments, I always obliged, even if I was "over the limit" for the week. My wife observed that I would probably always work full time for a church whether I was getting paid for it or not. It's just in my blood.

Even if I were to leave the full-time, professional pastorate, I know I would have to get immediately involved in some sort of teaching ministry in a local church. And I would have to keep writing books and articles like crazy. I would continue to study theology, try to interpret the Bible for today, and critique the church, the world, and my own life in light of the Word. Because, in the words of General Patton (from the movie), "I love it. God help me, I do love it so. I love it more than my life."

And that's perfectly okay.

ELEVEN

A God's-eye View

Vacation was winding down and—here's a real news flash—I didn't want to go back to work. I had been so relieved to spend a week with just my own family, instead of trying to squeeze in time with them around the lives of everyone else in my congregation. I started to wonder if maybe I'd like to find a different sort of job, nine to five, five days a week, so I could spend more quality time with my wife and kids. I also began to think of what awaited me back at work—the phone calls I would have to make, the meetings I would have to attend, the complaints I would have to hear. Is that really how I wanted to spend my life? Thinking about the church led me to attempt to evaluate my ministry. Was I really making a difference in my small church? Had the congregation moved forward under my leadership? Or was I, in fact, wasting my time and talents with this small group? Couldn't I be much more effective and accomplish a lot more if I were pastoring a larger church?

Luckily, before I talked myself out of turning my phones back on and returning to duty, I realized what I had been doing. Like so many small-churchaholics, I was concentrating on what I would like, what I wanted, and on my own assessment of the situation. But, as a Christian who claims that Jesus is *Lord*, the bottom line really should be what he likes, what he wants, and his assessment of the situation.

In America, we've lost the concept of lordship. We rebel against authority figures. We criticize our leaders. We laugh at sitcoms where precocious children talk back to their parents and teachers. We thumb our noses at our bosses by cutting corners at work. If we don't like our current jobs, we can escape by sending out applications and resumes, seeking another. In the Bible, however, people understood what it meant to have a supreme boss, an absolute monarch, a master, a lord. You wouldn't dare to question your sovereign. You, the slave, had to do what your owner said, no ifs ands or buts. You couldn't easily be released from your servitude. You had to make the best of it. Some slaves even chose not to obtain their freedom when they had the chance, but rather to dedicate their lives to pleasing good, loving masters.

I have a good, loving Master, and I want to dedicate my life to pleasing him. Therefore the question to be asked is not what do I think about my life and ministry, but rather, what does Jesus think about them?

What Jesus Thinks of the Church

How does Jesus look at your church? Fortunately, the answer is not as hard to obtain as it may at first seem. In the Bible, we have an account of Jesus evaluating churches. We can see exactly which congregations get a passing grade and which are in danger of failing. Although my book is not the place for an exhaustive study on Revelation 2–3, consider these few thoughts on the letters to the seven churches and use them to begin to see your congregation through Jesus' eyes. I think you'll see that small churches don't necessarily come out as poorly as some church-growth literature would lead us to believe.

The Church in Ephesus (Revelation 2:1–7). If this congregation was preparing a brochure touting the virtues of its history and ministry, it would have a lot to brag about. "We work hard for the Lord and never give up, even in the face of hardships. We're not afraid to stand firm for God's truth, even to the point of opposing those who have departed from the Word. We've kept our enthusiasm for the ministry. And we're not winding down, we're just getting started!" However, Jesus has another point of view. "You've lost something so important that if you don't recover it you will cease to exist as a church. You have lost your first love." Either the Ephesians had begun doing all their good deeds out of habit instead of out of love for Christ, or they had stopped loving each other in the way that Christ first loved them. In a busy, hard-working congregation that's easy to do. Tasks (especially fighting for the truth) become primary. Love is secondary. But not to Jesus.

The Church in Smyrna (Revelation 2:8–11). Their brochure would read: "We're a poor congregation. Not a lot of resources for ministry. Not a lot of avenues for ministry either because we are so persecuted by our community. In fact, our motto is, 'Join the Smyrna Evangelical Church—and die!' But we try to be faithful, come what may." And what words does Jesus have for them? "You only think you're poor. In my eyes, you're rich beyond measure!" What criticism does Jesus have for them? *Nothing!* Evidently Jesus didn't go to the modern management school which teaches that you've got to find at least one thing wrong with your subordinates or else they'll want a raise. (Actually, Jesus does offer them a raise. He's going to give them the crown of life!)

The Church in Pergamum (Revelation 2:12–17). "We live in an area that's hard to evangelize. Our town is a famous center for occult activity. Nevertheless, we try to be true to our Lord, even when our neighbors threaten us." Jesus says, "That's great! However, you also need to understand what holiness means. Some in your congregation evidently believe that they can be Christians while still essentially living a pagan lifestyle. Repent or face serious consequences!"

The Church in Thyatira (Revelation 2:18–29). "We're known for our good deeds, our stick-to-itiveness, and our deep love. In fact, you'll find that every day here is as exciting and meaningful as the time you first met Jesus!" However, that same Jesus himself says, "That's all well and good, yet you tolerate a false teacher who encourages your members to sin! I'm fed up! I gave this teacher time to repent, but she stubbornly refuses. Therefore, watch out! I'm coming in judgment and it's not going to be pretty!"

The Church in Sardis (Revelation 3:1–6). Their brochure would read, "Ask anyone in our area and they will tell you that our church is the place to be. We have an exciting, lively ministry." But Jesus said, "Lively? You're actually quite dead and you don't know it. Wake up! Believe and obey the Word. Start living holy lives or I will surprise you by bringing judgement on you when you least expect it."

The Church in Philadelphia (Revelation 3:7–13). "To be honest, we don't have a lot going for us. We don't have numbers or resources. Persecution has really cut down our ranks. Sometimes we wonder how much longer we can keep going. But we try to be faithful." Jesus responds, "Because you have been faithful, I am about to open doors for you and do more than you could possibly imagine. I love you and will show the world that I do!"

The Church in Laodicea (Revelation 3:14–22). "We're a congregation that has truly been blessed. We have all the resources we need and then some! We can easily keep funding our ministry for years and years to come." Jesus' famous response? (This time I'll quote directly from the Bible.) "I know your deeds, that you are neither cold nor hot. I wish you were either one or the other! So, because you are lukewarm—neither hot nor cold—I am about to spit you out of my mouth."

Pretend for a moment that you were church-shopping in the first century A.D. Based on the imaginary brochures and on what would be immediately obvious to human observers, which churches would you choose to visit? Be honest now. Wouldn't you check out Ephesus, Thyatira, Sardis, and Laodicea while giving Smyrna and Philadelphia a wide berth? Yet the latter two are the congregations that Jesus is really blessing even though they seem the most like failures in the eyes of the world.

Obviously Jesus doesn't judge the health, vitality, or potentiality of a congregation based on its level of activity, its financial and manpower resources, or its reputation as being an exciting, lively place to be. I wonder then why we do. Why do we automatically assume that the large congregation with the brand new building, the cutting-edge pastor, and the seven-days-a-week ministries is the place where God is *really* at work! Our tendency to jump to this conclusion has more to do with the fact that we live in success-oriented, "bigger is better," entrepreneurial America than it does with our being Bible-believing Christians.

It seems clear from a study of Revelation that Jesus is concerned with congregations learning to love him and their members, making the most of whatever limited resources they have, hanging on and being faithful in tough times, learning what it means to live holy lives, and depending utterly on Christ—not their strengths— for power, opportunity, and prosperity. Aren't these also the concerns of small churches that are seeking to follow Christ? As a small-church pastor, aren't you actually spending a lot of your time preaching, teaching, and working on areas that are vitally important to Christ? Doesn't Christ's agenda fit better with the "traditional" pastoral role so many small congregations expect the clergy to fill than with the CEO models advocated today? Could it be that Jesus is actually pleased with you and is blessing, or will soon bless, your ministry even though no national magazine will ever cite you as one of "The Ten Most Important Pastors of the Year?"[1]

But it often seems as though the small-church pastor has to work more on fixing the broken copier than on building the congregation up in love. You have to supervise the youth group's fund-raiser when you would rather be preparing a sermon on holiness. What about all the mundane, "busy work" tasks that we pastors are called on to do? How does Jesus view them? How should I view them?

Seeing Christ Behind Every Task

Think of those popular 3-D image pictures.[2] When you first glance at one of them, all you will see is rows and rows of ducks, balls, boxes, or whatever. In order to view the 3-D image you have to let the little rows of ducks blur, then the true picture which was there all the time underneath it all will emerge. (Or so I've been told—I can never get the crazy things to work.) Sometimes, as a pastor, I need to blur the seemingly endless lines of day-to-day tasks and ask myself, "Can I see Christ somehow behind them all?" Are those tasks resulting in Christ being portrayed and glorified to the congregation and the world? If so, then the tasks won't seem so bad. They certainly won't seem "worthless" or "a waste of time." Rather than distracting you from the real work of the ministry, they may actually be part of the real work of the ministry. Let me give you several examples of how this "blurring" process might work:

— Elderly Mrs. Jones calls requesting a pastoral visit. Though you say, "Yes," inwardly you scream, "No! No!" Mrs. Jones always rambles on about the way her family (in her mind) ignores and mistreats her. Also, she's just about stone-deaf and either doesn't hear or doesn't want to hear any words of actual counsel you have to give her. So it seems you'll have to go and "blow" another hour with her. Yet, isn't your presence with her reminding her that Christ cares for her? Doesn't she visibly calm down when you pray for her at the end of the visit even if you suspect she can only hear every fourth word you say? Could it be that Christ is ministering grace through you to her, your gritted teeth and stifled yawns notwithstanding?

— The custodian forgot to unlock the church for the Girl Scout troop that uses the fellowship hall on Tuesday nights. You get a call from them at home during supper. You race back to the church, grumbling all the way. (Hey! You're only human!) This is an imposition you didn't need during an already busy week. On the other hand, it's also a way to maintain good relations between the church and the community and let a few new folks meet the pastor. Opportunities to present the gospel to them may develop down the road. You're also modeling the servant leadership of Jesus and letting people see that the pastor is not "too big" to help them out.

— You find yourself mediating a quarrel between two factions over whether or not it's time to repaint the church stairs. Oh great! A chance to act as referee in the midst of petty bickering. Just what you always wanted. On the other hand, it is a chance to teach and model Christian love in a trying situation. And problems like these need to be hashed out and explosive emotions defused so that, on Sunday morning, the sanctuary will feel like hallowed ground and not a war zone. Christ isn't honored in a contentious atmosphere. Remember, too, that Jesus said, "Blessed are the peacemakers, for they will be called sons of God."

— Even if you have to type, copy, collate, and fold your own bulletins, you are working to facilitate worship for God's people. And you are bringing to their attention printed announcements about opportunities for service and growth. To be sure, the legitimate question needs to be raised, "Does the pastor really have to be the one doing this?" but, meanwhile, you shouldn't feel as though you are wasting your time in the office.

I'm not saying that there aren't such things as annoying interruptions and boring chores. There certainly are. There are even satanic interruptions from time to time. (For instance, it never fails that just when the ministry at Cobblestone starts to really take off, suddenly all the crazies in the community crawl out from the woodwork demanding my attention.) But in the midst of even these things, isn't God still at work? Not that he condones all the interruptions and tasks or even that he is behind them all, but isn't he finding a way to use them nonetheless for his glory? Romans 8:28 says, "And we know that in all things God works for the good of those who love him, who have been called according to his purpose." In all situations, we need to find the good that God is working and concentrate on that.

Dealing with Criticism

One area where it is hard for small-churchaholics to find the good is dealing with criticism. Criticism comes our way in the small church, not necessarily because smaller congregations are filled with cranky people (though some are), but because the small church is like a family. In a family, one freely voices concerns and wishes about how the home should be in a way one wouldn't voice concerns at something outside the home, like the local public library. Also, in a family, no outsiders better pick on us, but, boy, we sure can pick on each other! But, ironically, because the congregation is supposed to be one big family, when criticism comes your way it sometimes hurts even more. I thought these people loved me!

In the small church, every individual member's opinion assumes a great deal of importance. After all, we don't want to lose anybody! Members pick up on this and so feel quite free to let the pastor know their every complaint.

We know that God many times speaks to us through our brothers and sisters in Christ. But, how can we tell if a particular criticism is coming from the Lord or instead just from the troubled psyche of a parishioner? Is what we're hearing really God's perspective on our situation or not?

In the same chapter where he talks about controlling the tongue, James writes,

> Who is wise and understanding among you? Let him show it by his good life, by deeds done in the humility that comes from wisdom. But if you harbor bitter envy and selfish ambition in your hearts, do not boast about it or deny the truth. Such "wisdom" does not come down from heaven but is earthly, unspiritual, of the devil.... But the wisdom that comes from heaven is first of all pure; then peace-loving, considerate, submissive, full of mercy and good fruit, impartial and sincere (James 3:13–15, 17).

This passage gives us criteria by which to judge whether what we're hearing is from above or from down below.

The spirit in which criticism is offered is a very important clue. I remember one of the first pieces of criticism I ever received as a preacher. While I studied for the ministry, I served as pulpit supply during the summer months for the church I had grown up in. I was the hometown boy "made good" and so I usually received nothing but enthusiastic praise for my messages. But one Sunday morning, one of the elders asked to speak to me later on in the afternoon. Something was definitely up. I was very nervous about the meeting as I knew the man had a reputation of not suffering fools gladly. Imagine my surprise, then, when he came over to the house looking equally as nervous as I felt. He sweated, stumbled over his words, apologized profusely, and even cried as he finally got his message across. He said, "Steve, please don't take this the wrong way. I don't want to discourage you in the ministry or upset you in any way. God has given you a wonderful gift and I don't want to see you stop using it on my account. In fact, what I'm about to say is only my opinion and if you pray about it and the Lord shows you otherwise, that's fine with me. It's just that, I feel you've been using too many slang phrases in your sermons. [He gave me some examples.] I'm afraid that kind of language distracts some people, like me, from the great biblical exposition that you're doing. I'm telling you this because we're Christian brothers and we're supposed to be honest with one another and also because I love you. I hope you're not mad."

Of course not! How could I be? In fact, I praised the Lord for him! As I reflected on what he said (and I had to reflect on it because it was offered in such a biblical way that there was a good possibility it was from the Lord), I saw he was right. Slang in the pulpit coming from a young preacher didn't come across as funny; it came across as cocky and disrespectful. The congregation was a long-established one made up of a good number of middle-aged and elderly Dutch farmers. They simply weren't used to hearing a preacher talk that way. I changed some of my language and learned the important lessons of being sensitive to my listeners and becoming all things to all men in order that, by God's grace, I may serve some.[3]

By contrast, I have had people approach me with their faces red, their veins bulging and threatening to pop, their limbs trembling with rage, and their mouths wide open ready to spew forth venom. Others come with an "I know I'm always right and I'm going to set the pastor straight once and for all" attitude. Some try to push their own agendas onto me, and by extension, the congregation. I've even known a few who would confront me so that they could boast to others that they have put the pastor in his place. Although it's very hard for me (because as a small-churchaholic I take everything anybody says to me very seriously), I try to ignore these kinds of people and their comments. I believe God doesn't want me to dwell on their criticisms, but rather fight with myself in order to set them aside—because, according to James 3, these comments and complaints are straight from the pit.

Also straight from the pit is the belief that if we had God's per-spective on our lives and ministries, we'd end up even more dis-couraged than usual. As I pointed out in part one of this book, small-churchaholics come to believe the lie that every time we open the Bible, we're going to be brought face-to-face with our failures as pastors and the failures of our churches. So we stay away from God. We feel bad enough about ourselves already without a visit from the impossible-to-please Cosmic Taskmaster. We're looking for someone to cheer us up and God just doesn't seem to fill the bill.

However, I find that actually just the opposite is true. The more time I spend apart from God, the worse I feel. As I've been trying to show, when I run to God and try to see things his way, I'm com-forted. The more I listen to sources other than God, the more dejected, frustrated, and confused I get.

These other sources aren't always antagonists in the church either. Sometimes they can be well-meaning friends, scholars, experts, fellow-pastors, and Christian media workers who, unwit-tingly, send the implicit message that unless I'm involved in a cut-ting-edge, multi-staffed, megachurch ministry that always knows exactly what it is doing and why, I'm nothing in the kingdom of God. I need to remind myself that their voices are not the voice of the Lord.

Hear now the voice of the Lord:

"Blessed are the poor in spirit, for theirs is the kingdom of Heaven.

Blessed are those who mourn, for they will be comforted.

Blessed are the meek, for they will inherit the earth.

Blessed are those who hunger and thirst for righteousness, for they will be filled."

—Matthew 5:3–6

The LORD did not set his affection on you and choose you because you were more numerous than other peoples, for you were the fewest of all peoples. But it was because the LORD loved you and kept the oath he swore to your forefathers that he brought you out with a mighty hand and redeemed you from the land of slavery.

—Deuteronomy 7:7–8

The inspired apostle Paul wrote,

Here is a trustworthy saying that deserves full acceptance: Christ Jesus came into the world to save sinners—of whom I am the worst. But for that very reason I was shown mercy so that in me, the worst of sinners, Christ Jesus might display his unlimited patience as an example for those who would believe on him and receive eternal life.

—1 Timothy 1:15–16

Be shepherds of God's flock that is under your care, serving as overseers—not because you must, but because you are willing, as God wants you to be; not greedy for money, but eager to serve; not lording it over those entrusted to you, but being examples to the flock. And when the Chief Shepherd appears you will receive the crown of glory that will never fade away. . . . clothe yourselves with humility toward one another, because, "God opposes the proud but gives grace to the humble." Humble yourselves, therefore, under God's mighty hand, that he may lift you up in due time. Cast all your anxiety on him because he cares for you.

—1 Peter 5:2–7

"Come to me, all you who are weary and burdened, and I will give you rest. Take my yoke upon you and learn from me, for I am gentle and humble in heart, and you will find rest for your souls. For my yoke is easy and my burden is light."

—Matthew 11:28–30

Those don't sound to me like the words of a cruel slaver. Nor do they sound like the words of one ready to abandon small churches and their pastors. I'm going to try to believe these words.

How about you?

TWELVE

I'm Not the Messiah

Little children often get confused as to exactly who the pastor really is.

After I had mentioned dogs during one children's sermon, a three-year-old tugged at my robe and said, "Hey, God! Hey, God! Did you know I have a dog, too?"

Another little boy was caught stealing money out of our offering plate. His mom and dad wanted their son to confess his sin to me because, they said, "In his mind, you're right up there alongside God."

Each year our church throws a "Hallelujah Party" as an alternative to Halloween. People come dressed in costumes with biblical themes. Once I attended dressed in a gorilla suit (the theme was "The Animals on Noah's Ark") and inadvertently ended up scaring all the preschoolers. One little girl was hesitant about attending church after that party. When her parents wanted to know what was wrong, she asked them, "Jesus isn't going to be a gorilla again, is he?"

As a small-churchaholic, I can find myself thinking like a child. I can start to believe that I am Jesus. Now before you call the ambulance to haul me away in the nice white coat with extra-long sleeves, let me explain what I mean. I can easily start to view myself as being the savior of my congregation. My friends and I call it "The Messiah Complex." For example, I can feel that it's up to me to get the alcoholic to sober up. If he doesn't, of course, it means I failed.

There must have been something wrong with the counsel I gave him. Maybe I should have tried a different approach. I should have expressed the fact that I cared about him more often. At any rate, the reason the poor soul is still drowning his sorrows in booze is that I blew it. Saviors are supposed to save, after all.

If my church isn't growing numerically, there must be something wrong with my preaching. It's up to me to motivate my people to evangelize the world. I'm failing in my task again. I should have the power to change people's hearts and minds. Yet, my proposal gets shot down by the board. There must have been something wrong with my presentation. I need to revamp it and present it again at our next meeting. You see, the church's future all rises and falls on me. If anything good happens around here, it's because I had a hand in it. If things aren't right, it's because I'm not doing my job. The Lord is depending on me! And I dare not let him down! After all, doesn't the Bible teach that "we who teach will be judged more strictly" (James 3:1)?

Many of us who preach "salvation by grace alone" often act as though our works are what really counts when it comes to our relationship with God. The Lord demands perfection from his servants and anything less puts us in the hands of an angry God. Now, a concern for holiness is certainly commendable and even biblical, but it's also biblical that there was only one perfect human to ever walk the face of the earth—and I'm not him.

The Bible gives us examples of leaders who blew it, but were used by God again. Consider Moses. His first reaction to God's call was, "O Lord, please send someone else to do it" (see Exodus 4:13). Then, because Moses had not circumcised his son (a serious, covenant-breaking sin for a Hebrew), the Lord came to Moses and was actually about to kill him (4:24–26)! Yet, we all know the intimate relationship Moses came to have with the Lord and the ways in which God used Moses as deliverer, lawgiver, and prophet.

Consider Jeremiah, the prophet who once had the gall to accuse the Lord of deceiving him and tell the Lord that he wished he had never been born (Jeremiah 20:7, 14–18). Yet, God kept his promises to Jeremiah and continued to give him a prophetic ministry.

Consider John Mark, who deserted Paul and Barnabas on their missionary journey and later was the reason that the famous duo broke up (Acts 13:13; 15:36–41). Yet, he wrote one of the Gospels, was eventually recognized by Paul as being a valuable Christian worker (2 Timothy 4:11), and was a close associate of Peter (1 Peter 5:13).

Speaking of Peter: Not only did he deny Christ three times (Mark 14:66–72), but also, after having received a direct revelation from God that Gentiles were welcome into the Kingdom (Acts 10), he shunned them in favor of the Jews (Galatians 2:11–21). Yet, he was a rock on whom Christ built the church!

You see, the message of the Bible is that God's grace is greater than the sins of church leaders. Jesus' blood covered *their* sins. Jesus' blood covers *your* sins. Let Jesus be *your* Savior when you feel that you've blown it.

Failure Is Not a Sin

Of course, feeling as though you've blundered is not the same as sinning, although in the mind of the small-churchaholic the two are often equal. The small-churchaholic mistakenly holds him or herself accountable for things over which he or she has no control. We become upset that we aren't all-knowing and all-powerful. But there's only One who can change the hearts of rulers (Proverbs 21:1), heal the sick (Acts 3:12–16), bring people to repentance (Acts 11:18), enlighten men and women to spiritual truth (1 Corinthians 2:14), remove prejudice and selfishness and in their place put love (1 John 4:7–8), and grant supernatural peace to troubled hearts (Philippians 4:7). And guess what? You're not him.

Therefore, you can't patch up all the broken marriages and broken hearts that appear before you for counseling. You can't bring the fire of revival to your community, nor the light of renewal to your congregation. You won't be able to comfort all the grieving, nor take away the pains of the shut-ins. You aren't the one who can make warring factions in the congregation kiss and make up. You can't transform complainers into cheerful, willing workers. You can't force stingy people to give more to the Lord's work. And you certainly can't reverse the decline and decay that plague some small communities.

Your job is to bring a Christian presence into the lives of your people and teach them what God has to say about their situations. The rest is between them and the Holy Spirit. View yourself as being a spiritual Don King, a cosmic fight arranger and manager. Through your preaching, teaching, counseling, and guidance, you set up matches between God and your people. Then, you step back and watch as your people wrestle with the Lord. You can offer advice and encouragement to them during the bout. You can help heal the wounded among them afterward, but they are the ones who have to get in the ring. The fight is theirs and the Lord's. You can't control the outcome.

If some combatants want to dig in their heels and resist God when it would be easier, healthier, and better for them to give up during round one, that's their choice, not yours. You can yell, "Stay down! Stay down!" for all you're worth, but you can't stop them from struggling to their feet again. If during a different sort of match, some want to let go of the Lord before he blesses them, that's their fault, not yours. Your job is to coach them to hang in there, but if they ignore you and give up, the shame is theirs alone. And if, after the battle, some refuse to come to the Bible for healing medicine and won't listen to your expert analysis of what they did wrong and how to improve next time, the dreadful consequence that they will either spiritually bleed to death or continue to get their lights punched out by the Lord is on their heads, not yours.

The apostle Paul certainly felt that way. At the end of his life, knowing that he had done all he could to coach God's people, he said, "I have fought the good fight, I have finished the race, I have kept the faith. Now there is in store for me the crown of righteousness" (2 Timothy 4:7–8). He was able to say this even though two verses later he talks about Demas deserting him and in verses 14–16 he makes it clear that he was hurt by Alexander and by the fact that no one would come to his defense. Anyone reading through the New Testament knows some of Paul's churches had serious problems, yet he felt he had been faithful. He didn't say, "Not everyone is following Jesus, therefore I must have been a crummy missionary."

Paul knew that he was the Lord's herald and prophet. He was not the one expected to produce results. The disciples of Jesus also knew this. When Jesus sent them out to preach the kingdom of God, he warned that some would reject them. When that happened, he told them to shake the dust off their feet and move on. He didn't say, "Know this, that you have failed as ministers and are profitless servants." Neither did he say to them, "Keep hanging in there, trying every new technique you can possibly think of in order to turn things around." No, Jesus said to move on.

The Lord doesn't want our identity and self-worth as pastors to be bound up in results. This is good news for those of us ministering in small churches where results are hard to come by. But it's also hard news to accept while we live in a country where production, profits, gains, and "the bottom line" are all that seem to count.

Another reason why small-churchaholics have problems accepting this is that they often spend too much time with "the failures" and not enough time concentrating on "the successes." If I spend two hours a week for six months with a counselee (not to mention all those phone calls) and the person is no better off than when we started, of course I'm going to feel like a zero as a pastor. If I keep visiting someone's Uncle Ralph because "he really needs to know the Lord, Pastor," and he never responds to the gospel, I'll come to believe that I have no gifts in the area of evangelism. If I spend years preaching to a stubbornly dead (and proud of it) congregation, I'll conclude the Word of God has no effect when it comes out of my mouth. Instead of denigrating myself, the answer in these cases may be to shake the dust off my feet and move on to where the fields are white unto harvest. This is not an admission of failure, but it's a realization that some people are determined to oppose God until their dying day. I shouldn't waste my time on endeavors that the Lord clearly isn't behind.

It's hard for the small-church pastor to cut off counseling with individuals because of the possible consequences. The former counselee may do something stupid. The pastor may be blamed if the former counselee does something stupid. Also, because small churches are built on relationships, a feeling may arise among the congregation that you are distancing yourself from a parishioner, maybe even because secretly you don't like him or her. Aren't you being paid to be available to everyone? Aren't you supposed to be everyone's friend? There may also be unspoken dread on the part of some of the congregation that, if the troubled individual can no longer call and bug you endlessly with problems, he or she may start calling and bugging them! You've got to find ways to terminate the counseling without ending the relationship.

Why not say to the soon-to-be-dropped counselee, "I'm feeling bad that I don't really seem to be able to help you all that much. I would like you to try seeing Dr. Moretraining at the Christian Counseling Center over in Next Town. I've heard that she's an expert in dealing with the kinds of problems you have. Let's drive over together and check out the situation. And then from time to time let's get together over coffee and you can let me know how it's going." Or, "I don't think we're getting anywhere with this counseling approach. Let's try something different. I'm teaching a Bible study on Thursday evenings that deals with some of your concerns. I think you'll find during the discussions that the people attending understand what you're going through and that they've got a lot of wisdom and help to offer. I'd like to invite you to start coming on Thursday nights."

Of course, it helps if either your board has previously given you carte blanche when it comes to your pastoral counseling or else is willing to listen to your frustrations over certain counselees and give you their blessing to terminate the sessions. Then it's "Yeah, we all know Randy's never going to change and that he starts to get to you after a while," instead of "Why's the pastor suddenly being mean to Randy?"

When It's Time to Move On

When it comes to deciding to leave a congregation and shake the dust off your feet, small-churchaholics have even more of a problem. We desperately want everyone to like us and we know some will be very upset by our leaving (of course, others may throw a victory party). We tend to be guilt-ridden, too. We know that it takes time for anything to happen in a small church. Are we guilty of bailing out too early? We know that relationships are the key to ministry. Maybe we haven't been working hard enough on building them. We once believed that God called us to our present churches. What does our leaving say about our faith in him? How do we know that our situations are really hopeless? Maybe we're just tired or whining and complaining too much. Is the Lord leading us to greener pastures (Acts 16:6–10) or is it really Satan seducing us away from our true mission fields?

While we may know, at some level deep down inside, that one sure cure for insanity is to leave an insane situation, we find it hard to call U-Haul. While there's nothing biblically wrong with wanting to advance yourself and improve your lot in life (1 Corinthians 7:21) or moving on even if there are still needy people at your current call (Mark 1:36–39; 2 Corinthians 2:12–13), we still find it hard to start packing up our libraries. Here are five principles that have helped me take the drastic step in the past:

1. *When nobody else in your congregation seems to share your vision for the future, it's time to move.* It only takes a couple of allies (particularly if they are the right allies) in the small church to win the war. Unfortunately, sometimes you don't even have that. After trying everything I knew to energize a dying congregation, I suggested to the board that we participate in a church revitalization program offered by our denomination. To kick it off, we would have to go on a retreat with our synod executive. The members shifted uncomfortably in their seats. One finally spoke up, "I just don't think any of us wants to give up a whole weekend to do something like that." I believe the next day I had my resumé in the mail.

2. *Other pastors will confirm your decision to leave.* As a young pastor, I both longed for and dreaded the meeting I had set up with our clerk of classis. Even though I felt it was time for me to leave my current church and move on, I fully expected the older, more experienced man to counsel the youngster to show some guts and hang in there. Instead, he asked me, "What's your professional assessment of the situation in your church?" Imagine that—me, a professional! I told him and he responded by saying that, from what he knew about the church, he agreed with me. I felt as though I had received confirmation from the Lord and looking at it in retrospect, indeed I had.

3. *When your spiritual gifts don't match your current situation, it's time to move.*[1] Use one of the many diagnostic tools available to determine the gifts that God has given you. Even if you took such an inventory while attending seminary or Bible college, take one again now. During your years in ministry, God may have granted you new gifts, or the situations you have faced may have caused hidden gifts to emerge. Instead of answering the inventory questions on your own, invite your spouse, a close friend, or a trusted colleague to go through them with you. Others often notice qualities in your personality or discern the effects of certain aspects of your ministry that you cannot.

The body of Christ is built up as each part is respected for what it is (1 Corinthians 12) and for doing its appropriate work (Ephesians 4:16). What part of the body are you? What is your proper work? Make a list of the ways a person with your gifts should be spending his or her time. Imagine that a church or Christian organization is looking for someone just like you. Write down what you think that job description would look like. Now, examine your current call. List the activities in which you are engaged and the duties you perform in a typical week. How are you spending your time? Regardless of whatever the church leaders and members officially said to you in the past, what do they really want in a pastor? For example, they may have said during the candidating process that they want a pastor who emphasizes Bible study, but how many members actually attend the weekly studies? With all these things in mind, write a job description for your current position. Does it come close to your ideal one, or not?

Then, make a list of the top ten problems or challenges confronting your church in the immediate future. Input from denominational executives and from laypersons can be helpful here. (Do not tell your congregation's members that you are using this information to decide whether or not to move!) How could your gifts be used to help your congregation deal with these issues? Has the Lord equipped you in the areas in which the church needs help, or could these people be better served by someone with a different gift mix? If it becomes evident that you're a square peg in a round hole, you are free to leave to search out square holes! This process helped me find mine.

4. *Make sure you honestly evaluate a new call before accepting it.* More than once, I've realized that the churches I was offered were basically the same as the one I currently pastored, just with different names and faces. Moving would have gained me nothing. The writer of Ecclesiastes said, "There's nothing new under the sun." That includes small churches.

5. *Consider your family's needs as well as your own.* The Bible may tell us to put Christ ahead of everything, but it also says that "If anyone does not provide for his relatives, and especially for his immediate family, he had denied the faith and is worse than an unbeliever" (1 Timothy 5:8). I left one call partially because my family couldn't afford a safe place to live in the area. Can you continue to care for and support your family where you are now? Do you have children with special needs who could benefit from programs offered elsewhere? Are there any health considerations which would lead you to change climates? Finally, is your current ministry a joy or a burden to you all (Hebrews 13:17)?

Remember, the Lord didn't keep the proclamation of the Gospel confined to the sphere of the Jews who rejected it. He moved on to the Gentiles. If the Messiah, by his Holy Spirit, moves on, there will be times for you to move on as well. The servant isn't greater than the master. Follow the Master's lead.

THIRTEEN

The Only Thing to Fear
Is Fear Itself

Everything I ever needed to know I learned from Rush Limbaugh. Well, okay, maybe not everything, but one very important thing: self-reliance.

Regardless of what you think about Rush's politics or his radio program, you have to admit that he has a point when he says that too many members of our society view themselves as helpless victims of the powers-that-be or circumstances beyond their control. As a result, they will never try to improve their lot in life. Why bother? All such efforts are doomed to failure, anyhow, because the deck is too stacked against them. Instead, these "powerless" people sit around waiting for someone or something, usually the government or the courts, to step in and save them. When the powerless view the powerful in our society, they do so with disdain. The powerful don't deserve to be where they are. They haven't risen to the top because of ability or hard work, but because of favoritism or bribery or quirks of fate. "I can never be what they are. The best I can hope for is if the government takes some of what they have and gives it to me."

Sound familiar? It should. Rush could just as well be describing the small-churchaholic.

Many small-churchaholics view themselves as victims of the powers-that-be or circumstances beyond their control. They never planned on ministering in a small church, but they weren't polit- ically connected in their denominations and because there are so many small-church pulpits for the authorities to fill, that's where they were dumped. Some even view themselves as victims of God—after all, he's ultimately responsible for where they ended up. And certainly, they believe they are continually victimized by their congregations. Oh, they could stretch their wings and really fly, dazzle the world (and especially denominational headquar- ters) with their pastoral gifts and inspired leadership! But every time they advance new ideas, their boards say, "No," or some influential long-time members get upset, or the ideas prove to be impractical given congregational resources, or key people involved move away, and nothing goes anywhere.

About the time a small-churchaholic starts to work on exciting projects, Mrs. Brown's niece's brother-in-law goes in the hospital for major surgery and "Pastor, the family really needs you now!" So, many pastors give up trying to move their congregations ahead. The exciting ministries, the "cutting-edge" churches, the revivals, the better salaries, the accolades from peers, the advancements to "plum" assignments, the write-ups in national media, these are all for others, not for them. It's just never going to happen, no matter what they do. Their only hope is that some- day, some way, by some miracle, a denominational official (maybe a friend who has risen to the top) will take pity on them and let them in on the gravy train, too. Of course, with people like Bill Hybels, Rich Warren, and John Maxwell around, chances are that they won't be noticed or even remembered by the higher ups. And what's so great about Bill Hybels, Rich Warren, and John Maxwell anyway? "If they had been stuck in a congregation like mine, nobody would have ever heard of them! Those guys really lucked out!"

Well, small-churchaholic, prepare yourself for a shock. Bill Hybels, Rick Warren, and John Maxwell would probably do quite well pastoring your congregation, because they, like Rush, have tremendous faith in the gifts God has given them, work hard, and don't let fear of failure stop them from trying something new.

Listen as Rush himself speaks:

As the popularity of the Excellence in Broadcasting Network soars to new heights, reporters frequently approach me and ask, "Did you ever expect to rise to the top the way you have?" My answer is always the same: "Yes, of course. I was striving for it. I didn't move to New York just to be in the top five. My eye was always on Number One." The fact of the matter is that I've always been that way, ever since I was a little kid. I was never intimidated by the prospect of failure. I knew that if I missed the mark, I could live with myself. What I couldn't live with, however, was the prospect of not having taken my best shot at the brass ring.[1]

Most people have no idea how good they are—even people who are excellent at what they do. Do you know why? Because most people allow themselves to be shackled or constrained in some way. It might be the result of a self-imposed limitation, the restrictions of their job, or the responsibilities they've accepted.[2]

Don't kid yourself. I am fully aware of the very real problems our nation faces. But I would rather suggest answers and solutions and encourage people to take responsibility than to sit around and whine about how unfair the world is. That accomplishes nothing.[3]

Or if you don't want to listen to the one "with talent on loan from God," as Rush describes himself, then how about listening to God himself? While "God helps those who help themselves" may not be an exact quote from the Bible, it's a principle that is taught throughout the Scriptures. I once heard Steve Brown say on the radio that the message of the Book of Proverbs was, "Trust God and lock your doors." Waiting for God to act doesn't preclude us taking action ourselves and using our common sense.

In Acts 23, for example, when Paul gets wind of a conspiracy to assassinate him, he takes action to prevent it, even though the Lord had assured Paul that he would be all right in verse 11.

Philippians 2:12 urges us to "continue to work out your salvation with fear and trembling." Second Peter 1:5–8 commands us to "make every effort to add to your faith" those character traits which will keep us from "being ineffective and unproductive" in the Lord. First Corinthians 7:21 seems to indicate that while we must learn to be content where God has placed us, it's also all right to take advantage of any opportunities that come our way to advance ourselves. And Jesus said in Matthew 11:12, "The kingdom of heaven has been forcefully advancing, and forceful men lay hold of it."

So stop sitting around feeling trapped and hopeless. Stop spending your time whining to your spouse, your pastor pals, and God about your lot in life. Boldly step out in faith to take action to improve it—now! Don't worry about the possible consequences of taking action. You can't let fear cripple you. As a famous naval hero once said, "_____ the torpedoes! Full speed ahead!" Or as the author of Proverbs warns, "The sluggard says, 'There is a lion outside!' or, 'I will be murdered in the streets!'" Lazy people can always come up with reasons for doing nothing, usually based on fear. Unfortunately, they also start to believe their reasons and ultimately convince themselves that there's absolutely nothing they can do. Look out your window, small-churchaholic. There's no lion there, no murderer skulking about. Go on outside! The fresh air will do you good.

When Fears Are Unfounded

Let me share with you three dark times in my life when fear of torpedoes, lions, and tigers, and bears (Oh, my!) almost did me in.

I had been pastoring a congregation for less than a year, and already I knew it wasn't going to work out. Many of the key leaders and I weren't theologically compatible. My family was going into debt in order to continue ministering in the area. At the same time, there were grumblings in the church that, compared with the last pastor, I was already being paid too much. So I knew I had to get my resumé out and start it circulating. But voices from well-meaning friends and inside my own mind nearly stopped me.

"You haven't been here long enough to really give this church a chance," the voices said. "When a search committee sees that you've only been at this current call a short while, they will think there is something wrong with you—that you can't get along with people or that you want everything perfect. Are they really going to believe you when you explain to them why you want to move? Or are they going to want to hear your congregation's side of the story? Speaking of your congregation, if you think your life is miserable now, just wait and see what happens if they happen to get wind of the fact that you want out! No, better to stay put for a few more years so you can have a resumé that looks good."

The situation became so intolerable, however, that I felt forced to start actively seeking another call. Much to my surprise, churches in Michigan, Canada, Iowa, and New York expressed interest in me even though I hadn't been two full years pastoring my current church. My fears proved to be totally unfounded, and I eventually accepted a call to another congregation where the living situation was better and my theology embraced.

I have always wanted to be a writer, partly because, from an early age, people told me I had talent, but also, because whenever I shared my thoughts about the ministry with other pastors, they told me they were helped. Maybe God had given me a gift that could be used for his glory to help others. Certainly any extra money I could earn from writing would be a great help to the family of this small-church pastor. Yet I never seemed to be able to get myself started. It wasn't that I didn't have any ideas. Oh, no! I had dozens of them. Unfortunately, I also had dozens of fears. I don't have multiple degrees attached to my name so who would want to buy what I had to say? Could I handle getting rejection slips? In my life as small-church pastor wasn't I already rejected enough? When would I find the time to work on books and articles? Wouldn't I just end up with a bunch of half-finished projects? And I didn't even begin to know how to submit anything to a publisher! I just knew it would require too much effort and research to find out.

My fears would have seen to it that my writing remained an unfulfilled dream had not my synod sponsored a seminar on "Expanding Your Ministry Through Writing" led by Steve Burt. Even after I signed up for it, I didn't want to go. My fears asked me, "What's the use?" But my wife said to me, "If you don't check it out, you'll always regret it." Deep down inside, I knew she was right, so, dragging my heels all the way, I slowly made my way to the seminar. And was I glad I had! Not only was Steve's presentation inspirational and motivational, but also, he was either able to answer my questions about "the business" or direct me toward resources that could. Now, instead of being a frustrated writer, I'm a published author, and my writing is opening up opportunities for me to lead seminars and workshops for Church Growth Institute, National Evangelism Workshop, the American Baptists, and the United Methodists. All of this is happening while I yet remain a full-time small-church pastor. And all because I listened to Steve Burt and my wife when they said (long before a certain athletic footwear company), "Just do it!"

On the last day of a church-growth conference where I had been exposed to such excellent speakers as C. Peter Wagner, John Maxwell, and Conrad Lowe, I took a walk by myself. It was a time for reflection and for communing with God. I felt that the presentations had, in a sense, given me back my calling. Years of ministering in small congregations and serving as basically a "chaplain" for small groups of believers had dampened the fire that I once had for reaching the lost for Christ. Now, I was once again feeling challenged, excited, and compelled to do all I could do to take the gospel to the unchurched. Yet, at the same time, a tremendous sadness came over me. I knew that after the conference, I would be going right back into the same sort of ministry that had frustrated my calling in the first place. I returned to my motel room and had a good cry. I also had one of those rare and special encounters with the Lord which really can't be explained in words, so I won't try. Suffice it to say that I came away believing that God was guiding me into a new phase of my life and my ministry. I looked forward to the evangelistic opportunities and challenges that would open up in front of me.

But my next church was yet another small congregation. I remember trying to reconcile that longing I felt with the facts of my current charge while mowing the parsonage lawn. I knew the basic law, "he who tries to move a small church ahead is a fool" and its corollary, "he who changes anything in a small church is doomed." I realized that the small church is an entirely different animal than the cutting-edge churches where unchurched baby boomers and baby busters are being reached. My fears were telling me to settle once again into the "chaplaincy" role expected of me, not to make any waves, and hope for a more exciting ministry at my next port of call. My heart, however, was desperate to try to find a way to be a church-growth pastor in a small church.

I began reviewing in my mind what I knew from first-hand experience, and the experiences of my friends, about small churches. I did some research on small churches. I was determined to be intentional about my ministry—to know exactly what I was doing and why—not just to put out fires for the congregation. Out of all of this came the principles that I've outlined and elaborated in my first book. Following those principles has enabled Cobblestone, by the grace of God, to grow. In the four and one-half years I've been here we've added seventy-three official new members, most of whom were previously unchurched.

Small Churches Can Change

I don't want to bore or anger any who have already read my first book (I can hear it now: "Hey! What's this? I paid for a *new* book!"), but permit me to review a few of those principles in the hope that they will inspire you to start to turn your congregation around and fulfill your dreams. After you've worked up the courage to face down your fears and are ready to actually try some new things, these principles may provide a battle plan.

I learned that small churches can change when—

— *The impetus for change comes from the congregation itself and not from an outside expert (like the pastor).* I said to the board of Cobblestone, "Many members have expressed to me their desire to see Cobblestone grow," not, "I'm a church-growth pastor and I'm here to lead you into the promised land." I said, "Some people are asking me if we couldn't include some of the more contemporary praise-worship songs in the service," not, "I've been reading that churches without praise-worship music are dying!"

— *Everybody has a hand in implementing the change.* I learned to be a "problem presenter" and not a "problem solver." I tell the board what's going on in the congregation and then let them decide what to do about it. I offer my input as merely "one of the gang," not as Super Leader or Numero Uno Dictator.

— *The change fits the congregation's existing identity and helps make it the best it can be.* You can easily lead a congregation of senior citizens to start programs that will reach out and meet the needs of the over-sixty-five residents of a community. You cannot get them to start a seeker-sensitive service geared toward Generation X.

— *Enough time is given for everyone to contemplate and feel comfortable with the change.* Sometimes I will plant some seeds in people's hearts before proposing a major change. I may drop a few comments like, "Lack of parking can be a real stumbling block to newcomers." I might pass out some church-growth literature for the board to read which has a paragraph or two in it about parking. I can point out during a few board meetings that parking has been kind of tight lately. And when the proposal is finally made, I'll go ahead and let the board debate, for months if necessary, exactly how to expand the parking lot and pay for it. If I want it done tomorrow, or worse, if the board makes a rush decision to do it tomorrow, we're in trouble. One day soon somebody's going to wake up and shout in shock, "Oh, no! What have we done? We've changed too much too fast!" My board has learned the value of tabling certain discussions and giving everyone a chance to "sleep on it."

I also learned that small churches can grow if—

— *They target friends, family members, neighbors, and co-workers.* The small church is suspicious of strangers, so don't invite any. Don't try to reach "the community." Reach people you know. At Cobblestone, we plan events that our members would feel very comfortable inviting their friends to. We've asked, "What kind of topics or programs would address the needs of the unchurched people you know and love?"

— *New blood is offered to go along with new ideas.* Leaders in a small church are often overworked and tired. They may turn down evangelism proposals if it seems that they are the ones who will wind up doing the bulk of the work. Try to get other members of the congregation to come on board even before you present your idea to the leadership. Then you can say to the elders, deacons, or trustees, "Here's what we'd like to do and here are the people who are willing to do it."

— *Fear of losing intimacy is addressed and dealt with.* I try to assure Cobblestone that I like small churches, I grew up in a small church, some of my best friends are in small churches. I have no desire to destroy the "family feeling" that exists here. As we grow, we will need to provide plenty of fellowship opportunities and small groups so people will have chances to get to know one another. We won't grow by expanding our sanctuary, but rather by going to multiple services, so that everyone will always have a regular "small congregation" they worship with on Sunday mornings.

— *Prayer is being offered for growth.* It never ceases to amaze me (O ye of little faith!) that we get a steady stream of visitors at Cobblestone who have no apparent existing connections to any of our members. People come through our doors because "Something was telling me that it was time to start attending church and for some reason I felt that this would be the one for me," or "We've always wondered what the little church on the hill was like." God is definitely answering the prayers of those in our congregation who are asking him for growth.

— *Effort is made to maintain an environment conducive to growth.* In some small churches, the tension in the air is so thick you could cut it with a knife. The Smith's aren't speaking to the Jones', or the newcomers are at war with the old-timers. When I preach sermons on forgiveness and acceptance, teach Bible studies on how the church should be different from secular organizations, and help the board to deal with delicate discipline problems, I am working toward growth every bit as hard as if I was doing a demographic study of our neighborhood.

Other Challenges

Let me briefly touch on some other challenging areas for the small-church pastor and give you some thoughts that might be helpful in formulating a plan of action. I don't claim to have all the answers, but maybe these ideas can stimulate your own thinking.

Personal and Church Finances

Find an advocate within the congregation. You usually cannot ask your board for more money without seriously undermining your ministry. "I knew it! The pastor doesn't really care about us. He or she is only in it for the money." "The pastor preaches a lot about sacrifice, but doesn't seem willing to do it." "Doesn't our pastor know how hard it is for a congregation our size to afford a minister today?" Instead, you need to find a trustworthy friend, an ally, that you can confide in. Then let the ally go to the board and say, "I think our pastor may be hurting a little financially. Can we do anything to help? After all, we want to take seriously our responsibility to meet the pastor's needs and we would hate to lose him or her."

Go ahead and take that part-time job. We small-churchaholics worry that the church family will get upset with us if, when they need us, we are slinging hamburgers down at the local diner. But it could just be that the small-church family will be relieved that you are trying to take care of your own problems without burdening them. Besides, if they get upset enough about you having to "moon-light," maybe they will increase your salary so you won't have to. Remember, too, that a "tent-making" ministry certainly has biblical warrant (Acts 18:1–4; 1 Thessalonians 2:7–9).

Conduct a stewardship campaign. Families don't like to talk about money and small-church families are no exception. It's a sore subject. But Jesus and Paul didn't hesitate to talk about money and we shouldn't either. Congregations will respond well if the focus of the campaign is on biblical teaching and on the need for Christians to give out of cheerful hearts in gratitude toward God.[4] They will rebel if they are told that the reason the campaign is being conducted is that "we need more money to meet our budget." This can lead to endless discussions about whether the budget is realistic, where we can trim it, etc.

Help the leaders to draft a clear mission statement for your congregation (Appendix 4 in my first book would be helpful here). Let the congregation know what your church is really all about and what sort of ministry the Lord is calling you to together. People can get excited about giving to a ministry, a mission, or a cause. People won't work up much enthusiasm for giving just so that an organization can survive for another year.

Run some fund-raisers. While a few may view bazaars, rum-mage sales, and pancake suppers as being non-Christian, believ-ing instead that a church's sole income should be from the tithes, gifts, and offerings of its members, there's nothing biblically wrong with the idea. In Exodus 12:35–36, the nation of Israel took "money" from the Egyptians. In Acts 4:34–37, we read about the practice of selling one's personal property and giving the proceeds over to the church. Can't a bunch of Christians get together and sell some things and turn the proceeds over to the church today? Besides, a fund-raiser can serve as an outreach to the community. The poor appreciate the low prices you offer at a yard sale. At a dinner, free church brochures can be lying around or perhaps a "homemade" video tape on the church's ministry can be playing in the area where people are waiting to be seated. Fund-raisers also give the members of your congregation a chance to spend time together, working side-by-side, getting to know one another. They can be good "body-building" activities.

Career Advancement

Get involved in Christian projects outside of your congregation. Even if the church you're serving doesn't have much going on in the way of ministry, you can still be involved in exciting works of God. Volunteer to do some work for a parachurch organization in your area or for your denomination. Other Christians will get a chance to see your gifts in action and may be able to serve as references for you in the future. You can add many experiences to your resumé instead of promoting yourself solely as a small-church pastor.

Consider making a career out of being solely a small-church pastor. Hopefully by now, if you've been paying attention as you read the rest of this book and have been listening to God, you've come to the conclusion that there's no shame in pastoring small congregations. In fact, there are many blessings and benefits. Instead of seeking to escape small-church ministry, why not make it your aim instead to become the best small-church pastor you can possibly be? For one thing, you'll probably never hurt for work. There are an awful lot of small churches out there.

Dealing with Problem People

Enlist them to fight for your causes. If certain types of individuals are going to go through life fighting, why not have them fight for you? Plant seeds of change in their hearts and minds. Give them books and articles to read about church growth and ask them their opinions on what they read. Bring a problem in the church to their attention by saying, "Don't you think something should be done about thus-and-so? Do you have any ideas about how we should handle it?"

Work for church growth. If you have people who enjoy being "big fish in a little pond," make the pond bigger. Their influence, power, and presence will shrink.

Try to maintain a relationship with those who disagree with you. Small churches usually expect or fear that their pastors aren't going to stay around very long. Why not surprise, shock, and even relieve many in your congregation by telling them that you'd like to be in it with them for the long haul? Approach trouble-makers with, "Isn't there some way we can work out our differences so that we can continue to minister here together?" Take the trouble-maker out for coffee. The bluster of many a trouble-maker fades in a one-on-one, friendly, informal setting. Remember Proverbs 15:1, "A gentle answer turns away wrath ..."

Purpose in your heart to ignore them. Some rabble-rousers are very influential members of the community. Others, though, are just "crazy uncles" or "nagging aunts" that the "family" tolerates with a sigh. When dealing with the latter, just smile politely as they bring you their latest complaints and say, "I'm sorry you're so upset," and then go ahead and do whatever it is you want to do anyway.

Take power away from them. Form new committees to deal with particular aspects of church life. Recruit new members for your board. Set up new "chains of command" in the church. Slowly but surely move your congregation away from doing things "because Ralph says so."

Make them part of the solution. When they gripe about something, say, "You're right. Can I count on you to write up a proposal to the board on what to do about it? Would you like to head up a task force to deal with it?" They will either back down or soon be too busy to bug you.

Practice church discipline. Notice I said "church discipline" not "pastor discipline." Unless the members of your congregation or your leaders are as fed up with the problem people as you are and see them as the threats to the ministry that you do, you will destroy your pastorate by confronting them. "Don't disagree with the pastor or he will fall on you like a ton of bricks. He's so sensitive and opinionated." "Did you hear how Pastor Marcia lost her cool with Bob the other day? Shouldn't a pastor be able to control her temper?" "Some people in this church really rub the pastor the wrong way." For biblical warrant for church discipline see Matthew 18:15–17, 1 Corinthians 5, and Titus 3:10–11.

I'm not foolish or presumptuous enough to try to dictate to you what you should do in your particular situation, but I do know that you must do *something*. Sitting around in hopeless despair because things are never going to change is a self-fulfilling prophecy. Waiting for things to turn around by themselves some-how, as if by magic, is living in a fantasy world. Refusing to make any effort to improve your life and congregation out of fear of fail-ure is cowardice, laziness, and an abandonment of your calling. Blaming everyone and everything else for your small-churcha-holism is abdicating personal responsibility.

Step out in faith and trust in the God who loves you. Gaining control of your church is leadership. Taking the reins of your life brings dignity and adventure.

In the words of another radio talk-show host, Dr. Laura Schles-singer, "Now, go take on the day!"

Bibliography

Bierly, Steve R. *Help for the Small-Church Pastor: Unlocking the Potential of Your Congregation.* Grand Rapids: Zondervan, 1995.

_____. "Lonely in a Close-Knit Church." *Leadership* 16, no 2 (Spring 1995): 98–100.

_____. "Navigating the Winters of Our Discontent." *Net Results* (February 1996): 16–17.

Burt, Steve. *Activating Leadership in the Small Church: Clergy and Laity Working Together.* Valley Forge, PA: Judson Press, 1988.

Corey, Melinda, and George Ochoa. *The Dictionary of Film Quotations.* New York: Crown, 1995.

Douglas, J. D., ed. *Dictionary of the Christian Church.* 2d ed. Grand Rapids: Zondervan, 1978.

Foltz, Nancy T. *Caring for the Small Church: Insights from Women in Ministry.* Valley Forge, PA: Judson Press, 1994.

Gilbert, Larry. "Lead or Get Out of the Way?" *Leadership* 16, no. 3 (Summer 1995): 126.

Larkin, William J. *Acts.* Downers Grove, IL: InterVarsity Press, 1995.

Limbaugh, Rush H., III. *See, I Told You So.* New York: Pocket Books, 1993.

McBurney, Louis P. "Prescription for Burnout Prevention." *Net Results* (March 1996): 19, 32.

Mead, Loren B. *More Than Numbers: The Way Churches Grow.* New York: The Alban Institute, 1993.

Miller, Keith A. "From The Editor." *Leadership* 17, no. 3 (Summer 1996): 3.

Norris, Kathleen. *Dakota: A Spiritual Biography.* New York: Houghton Mifflin, 1993.

Ortberg, John. "What's *Really* Behind Our Fatigue?" *Leadership* 18, no. 3 (Spring 1997): 108–13.

Oswald, Roy M. *Clergy Self Care: Finding a Balance for Effective Ministry.* New York: The Alban Institute, 1991.

Rovin, Jeff. *The Encyclopedia of Superheroes.* New York: Facts on File Publications, 1985.

Sanford, John A. *Ministry Burnout.* Louisville, KY: Westminister/John Knox Press, 1982.

Smedes, Lewis B. *Shame and Grace: Healing the Shame We Don't Deserve.* San Francisco: Harper Collins, 1993.

Smith, Charles Merrill. *How to Become a Bishop Without Being Religious.* New York: Pocket Books, 1965.

Stabbert, Bruce. *The Team Concept: Paul's Church Leadership Patterns or Ours?* Tacoma, WA: Hegg Bros. Printing, 1982.

Wagner, C. Peter. *Your Church Can Be Healthy.* Nashville: Abingdon, 1979.

Notes

Chapter Two: Tempests in a Teapot

1. Kathleen Norris, *Dakota: A Spiritual Geography* (New York: Houghton Mifflin, 1993), 62.

Chapter Four: We're Not in Kansas Anymore

1. See my book *Help for the Small-Church Pastor: Unlocking the Potential of Your Congregation* (Grand Rapids: Zondervan, 1995) for some ideas.

2. Kevin A. Miller, "From the Editor," *Leadership* 17, no. 3(Summer 1996), 3.

3. Larry Gilbert, "Lead or Get Out of the Way," *Leadership* 16, no. 3(Summer 1995), 126.

4. Unless, of course, one of these gentlemen is reading this book right now. In which case—you are he.

5. Loren B. Mead, *More Than Numbers: The Way Churches Grow* (New York: Alban Institute, 1993), 40.

6. C. Peter Wagner, *Your Church Can Be Healthy* (Nashville: Abingdon, 1979), 28–50.

7. Mead, *More Than Numbers,* 41.

8. William J. Larkin, Jr., *Acts* (Downers Grove, IL: InterVarsity Press, 1995), 82.

9. Wagner, *Your Church Can Be Healthy,* 88–100.

Chapter Five: Get a Life

1. See chapters 3 and 4 in my book *Help for the Small-Church Pastor* (Grand Rapids: Zondervan, 1995).

Chapter Six: Who Was That Masked Man?

1. I wonder how many *real* pastors actually spend hours each day in prayer? Why is it that in every ministerial fellowship I've attended,

the number one complaint of pastors, "My prayer life isn't what it should be"? Who determines "what it should be" anyway?

2. This is not to say that we should not grow in our ability to pray, but that we don't have to wait until we have attained some mystical level of perfection to talk to the Lord. Personally, I am looking forward to learning about prayer as communion, a way of just being in the presence of God.

Chapter Seven: Pastor Yourself

1. Nancy T. Foltz, *Caring for the Small Church: Insights from Women in Ministry* (Valley Forge, PA: Judson Press, 1994), 24, emphasis added.

2. You might be wondering how this sentiment matches up with the last chapter's emphasis on finding partners in ministry. All I can say is that life is full of contradictions and at least this one is biblical: "Carry each other's burdens, and in this way you will fulfill the law of Christ. . . . Each one should test his own actions. Then he can take pride in himself, without comparing himself to somebody else, for each one should carry his own load" (Galatians 6:2, 4–5).

3. Even if I am forced to give these things "a lick and a promise," as a pastor I will still spend more time dealing with God's Word than the average believer. Let's suspend belief for a moment and assume that the people in our congregations are spending a half-hour a day in the Bible. That would still be only three and a half hours a week!

4. For this concept I am indebted to Douglas Stuart, professor of Old Testament at Gordon-Conwell Theological Seminary.

Chapter Eight: Fragile — Handle With Care

1. John A. Sanford, *Ministry Burnout* (Louisville: Westminster/John Knox Press, 1982), 19.

2. If sex doesn't do these things for you and your spouse, consider getting counseling or, at the very least, reading several Christian books on marriage and sex. It's that important.

Chapter Nine: Two-Timing the Day-Timer

1. Nancy T. Foltz, *Caring for the Small Church: Insights from Women in Ministry* (Valley Forge, PA: Judson Press, 1994), 16.

2. If you are a layperson, you probably think I'm making this up. If you are a pastor, you know better.

3. And you had better believe that when I do, I check off the appropriate items on my weekly list.

Chapter Ten: To Thine Own Self Be True

1. Chuck Dixon, "Choice of Weapons," *Detective Comics* (October 1994), 13.

Chapter Eleven: A God's-eye View

1. Loren B. Mead, in his book *More Than Numbers: The Way Churches Grow* (New York: Alban Institute, 1993), points out that there are other means besides numerical growth for evaluating whether or not God is at work in a local congregation. Churches can grow in maturity, in community building, and in incarnating Christ to their community.

2. I heard this illustration in a sermon preached by the Reverend Janet Meyer Vincent of Living Springs Community Church in Saratoga Springs, New York.

3. Ironically, now I use slang again, but only because I am older and my audience has changed. At Cobblestone I preach to a lot of unchurched seekers, and it is important that I speak their language.

Chapter Twelve: I'm Not the Messiah

1. The following is adapted from Steve R. Bierly, "Navigating the Winters of Our Discontent," *Net Results* (February 1996), 16–17.

Chapter Thirteen: The Only Thing to Fear Is Fear Itself

1. Rush H. Limbaugh III, *See, I Told You So* (New York: Pocket Books, 1993), 12.

2. Ibid., 14.

3. Ibid., 16.

4. For an excellent program, consider the "Consecration Sunday" materials available from Cokesbury in Nashville at 800–672–1789 or 615–749–6113.

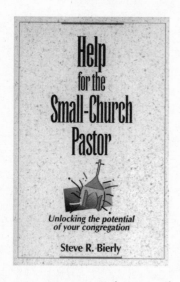

We want to hear from you. Please send your comments about this book to us in care of the address below. Thank you.

GRAND RAPIDS, MICHIGAN 49530

www.zondervan.com